Pass That Test

Our Additional Evidence-Based Resource Books for Educators

Handbook on Effective Instructional Strategies: Evidence for Decision-Making
Myles I. Friedman and Steven P. Fisher

Ensuring Student Success: A Handbook of Evidence-Based Strategies
Myles I. Friedman

Educators' Handbook on Effective Testing
*Myles I. Friedman, Charles W. Hatch, Jacqueline E. Jacobs,
Aileen C. Lau-Dickinson, Amanda B. Nickerson, and
Katherine C. Schnepel*

No School Left Behind: How to Increase Student Achievement
Myles I. Friedman

Effective Instruction: A Handbook of Evidence-Based Strategies
Myles I. Friedman, Diane H. Harwell, and Katherine C. Schnepel

Developing Teaching Effectiveness
Myles I. Friedman, Diane H. Harwell, and Katherine C. Schnepel

Developing Teaching Effectiveness: Instructor's Manual
Myles I. Friedman, Diane H. Harwell, and Katherine C. Schnepel

Pass That Test

A Guide to Successful Test Taking

Charles W. Hatch

THE INSTITUTE FOR EVIDENCE-BASED
DECISION-MAKING IN EDUCATION, INC.

Library of Congress Control Number: 2008926141
ISBN: 978-0-9666588-7-3

First published in 2008

The Institute for Evidence-Based Decision-Making in Education, Inc.
A South Carolina non-profit corporation
P.O. Box 122, Columbia, SC 29202

Printed in the United States of America

The paper used in this book complies with the
Permanent Paper Standard issued by the National
Information Standards Organization (Z39.48–1984).

10   9   8   7   6   5   4   3   2   1

Dedicated to all my
wonderful girls and David.

Contents

Preface

This volume is the result of the decades that I have conducted test preparation in many settings for vastly different audiences. My approach is to empower students to master tests that are frustrating to many. A thoughtful process that focuses on developing underlying skills and basic understanding is the best approach, as opposed to the more common approach of relying on item drill.

My first experiences in preparing persons to take standardized tests were in 1969 and 1970 on the Standing Rock Sioux Reservation in North Dakota. I was asked by the tribe to lead a number of classes for the General Educational Development (GED) test. Some of the lessons I learned in those first hesitant attempts are still part of the successful work that I do today.

The primary target audience for this book is administrators who have program responsibility for test preparation. They may be at the college level, with a focus on the Graduate Record Examination (GRE), Medical College Admission Test (MCAT), Law School Admission Test (LSAT), or PRAXIS. Other administrators may be at the school or district levels, with concerns and responsibility for the SAT, American College Testing Assessment (ACT), or state-mandated standardized tests.

The next target group is educational practitioners who have direct responsibility for test preparation at any level and who want to give classroom or tutorial activities a more productive focus.

The last audience is the broadest: it is parents and students who wish to increase standardized test performance at any level. This last group will want to focus on the practical approach features that follow and, most particularly, on the anecdotal examples. The first two groups will also be interested in the more detailed professional support segments.

A further effect of improved test preparation is a decrease in the dropout rate. If a school or college is able to increase the efficiency of instruction, student performance will increase and fewer students will find themselves so far behind that dropping out seems their only option. An added benefit will be better school and college performance on tests, which in turn becomes a powerful attractive force.

Let's compare two college programs. The first has never had a student fail the PRAXIS. Each student who prepares to take it is carefully groomed, prepared, and encouraged. There is also considerable pressure *not* to become the first failure; that is a distinction no one wants. The second has an occasional student pass; in fact, there was a period of about five years where only one student did so (there was a minor celebration when he did). For the first program success was the norm, while for the second program failure was the norm. In which program would you choose to enroll your child or grandchild?

I have been told many times by college students that, because of a failure to pass the PRAXIS, they had to drop out of college or change majors. There were no more courses that they were allowed to take, so attendance was just a waste of money. Desperate parents come to me because their child has dropped out and the student loans have come due. That really gets their attention.

How many superb athletes cannot pursue careers because of an inability to do well on the SAT or ACT? Some timely assistance would have made great differences in their careers. Make no mistake, this preparation process is not simple or easy, but this volume outlines my thoughts. A school can adopt as much as possible and pinpoint students who would benefit.

Sometimes poor test performance warps careers. I see many students who come to me after college for PRAXIS test help who have majored in such areas as psychology or child development only because they could not gain entrance into an education program. Then, after getting that unwanted degree, they decide to teach. Several have come to me to prepare for special education but have a psychology or sociology degree. It would have been so much better to pass the entrance test, take the special education courses, and learn the field. As it is, they really know almost nothing about the field in which they wish to be certified. Preparation is daunting.

OTHER PROFESSIONAL PREPARATION MATERIALS

Publishers have made a great deal of money from the publication of preparation books aimed at a particular test. Probably the most popular have been those books focused on the SAT and ACT. Over the past few decades, the series by Barron's is illustrative of a regularly updated series focused on one test. Like most others, it is a large-format, thick paperback. All kinds of other standardized tests have commercially prepared materials: post office exams, registered nurse exams, medical specialty exams, LSAT, GRE, and so on. Usually a short section containing general advice and tips is included. One volume that seemed to offer generalized preparation help was *Guide to Standardized Test Preparation* (Hawkes, 1999), but in fact the book is focused only on the special education student in middle and high school. Another pair of books in the Cliffs series (Bobrow, 1985; Covino and Orton, 1986) focuses on a variety of tests by broad categories: verbal and math. Both of these are helpful but miss the present volume's depth of focus.

For decades, the foremost test developer, the Educational Testing Service (ETS), maintained that coaching or test preparation courses, especially for the SAT, had no measurable effect on scores. Part of the basis for this viewpoint lay in their insistence that the test measured deep academic proclivities and thus was not liable to any change through short preparation sessions. Then, in the 1990s, when their own research began to show a measurable effect, they changed their viewpoint. The ETS report by Donald Powers and Donald Rock (1998) shows clearly the conflict of two viewpoints. On the basis of the analysis of scores of some 4,000 test takers, 500 of whom had been coached, they concluded: "The various analyses produced somewhat different . . . estimates. All of the estimates, however, suggested that the effects of coaching are far less than is claimed by major commercial test preparation companies." They estimated the coaching effect as eight points on verbal and eighteen points on math. Coincidentally or not, ETS began to publish their own extensive test preparation materials. The ETS Web site (www.ets.org) provides an extensive array of preparation materials for purchase.

The process that I will discuss is both demanding and extensive. It is demanding on both the instructor and the student because my approach requires the devotion of time and effort. In the world of high-dollar business consulting, the same kind of demand holds true. When a consulting group is brought in to turn a company around, the solution is never simple. Most often the company just wants a simple suggestion of a machine, a computer program, or a short training process. They desire a fundamental change in the bottom line without making fundamental changes in how they do business.

The least successful implementations are always the ones where the change is most limited. For years, General Motors (GM) engaged consultants who called for fundamental changes in corporate culture and the way the company did business. One GM board member, Ross Perot, called for the same kind of change. Not coincidentally, he came to GM from outside the automobile industry, from one of the most innovative areas of commerce, the computer industry. His company, Electronic Data Systems (EDS), was bought out by GM, hoping that the infusion of technology and innovative personnel would help. His constant calls for fundamental change were so troubling that he was finally bought out and forced to give up his seat on the board. A decade later, with no fundamental changes implemented, GM is in such serious trouble that its continued existence is in doubt. These troubles have been largely caused by its unwillingness to make the kind of changes that have been called for since the 1980s.

Test preparation is actually very similar. A school that just wants to add a bit of preparation time to what they already do incorrectly will not see much change. The refocusing required is both fundamental and difficult. I am reminded of a student I had a few years ago. After the first class, where I outlined the structure of the process to improve test scores, she asked me whether I really wanted to change everything about her. I said that I did. She was thinking about what I had said about health changes (sleep, nutrition, and exercise) as well as such fundamental skills as vocabulary, reading speed, and comprehension. I was pleased that she had really "heard" me. Also, bear in mind that some institutions and individuals are just like GM—they want the benefits without making painful, demanding changes. Life just doesn't work that way.

Another example will help clarify the dilemma. Some years ago I was called into a middle school to make suggestions to improve the students' dismal standardized test scores. I found that the classroom testing was, without exception, on the knowledge level of Bloom's Taxonomy. (The taxonomy provides educators with a scale in graduated complexity from Knowledge at the low end to Evaluation on the high end.) Every one of the thousands of test questions that I saw involved simple recall of information. When these children were asked questions on a standardized test requiring a demonstration of understanding, application, or analysis, they were lost because they had so little experience with those levels of understanding. Along with the low level of the questions, the teacher-given tests focused on very small segments. For example, a classroom test might deal only with capitalization or with adding fractions. However, the year-end standardized test would mix all kinds of questions together. The children did well on a test where they could attend only to the capitalization rules or the fraction addition rules, but poorly on a test where many concepts were mixed because they did not really understand and were not expected to understand. The teachers were very resistant and even hostile to my analysis and diagnosis because the remedy would cause them to rethink every lesson they taught in every subject. Just like GM.

Successful test preparation must address deep skills or face failure. Dealing with surface issues and practicing items are two very inefficient methods. In 2006 a North Carolina student came to me for assistance with two tests in the elementary education field (PRAXIS 0011 and 0012). One was in a multiple-choice format and the other an essay format, but both involved the same material. Both included all subjects taught in elementary schools (reading, language arts, math, science, social studies, art, music, and physical education). Sadly, she failed to make the North Carolina required score by a considerable margin. The score report contained a listing of all the PRAXIS tests she had taken. Previously she had failed both the PRAXIS I reading and math by considerable amounts. After these failures she did not work to remediate but switched majors. Then, when she took the more advanced tests, she failed because she had never addressed her basic skill weaknesses in reading and math. Analysis of the last scores showed low performance overall (reading problems) but especially on math, where her reading weaknesses were compounded by math shortcomings. Successful preparation in her case meant stepping backward to address those two basic weaknesses with long, involved instruction to reach the point where she understood both well. I am not sure that she was willing to undertake that slow, demanding process.

Another example will help clarify the benefit of addressing basic skills and underlying structures in a preparation program. Several years ago my best friend was diagnosed with cancer. After his operation he began chemotherapy. During one of his visits, his doctor told him of a problem she was having with the board exam for national certification in hematology and oncology; she had failed a number of times. He suggested that I might be able to help, so we began meeting for about an hour when she could schedule it. We met about six times for a total of five or six hours. We concentrated on increasing reading speed, raising comprehension, and understanding test item structures. I certainly could not review the content material of the test; I simply do not know much at all in that area. She passed.

In 1982 I conducted my first workshop preparing a group of teachers to pass what was then called the National Teachers Exam (NTE) (now called PRAXIS). This class was the product of a question I was asked at church by a good friend who had been unsuccessful in passing the NTE in elementary education for ten years; she wanted to know if I knew anything about that test. I answered in the affirmative for two reasons. First, I had taken several forms of the NTE with success as a teacher myself. Second, I was just completing my Ph.D. in Educational Research from the University of South Carolina, where I had learned about testing from a more theoretical point of view. That first NTE workshop was no great success from the participant point of view because only one person passed out of twenty. However, it was successful for me because I began to see how to focus the preparation and incorporate elements that would increase scores for more people. From the beginning, I only offered NTE/PRAXIS workshops on a guaranteed basis; students who failed received a refund. This single feature was a powerful impetus for me to refine the process to raise the passing rate by continuously refocusing the presentation and materials. Shortly the pass rate rose to about 85 percent, where it has remained for decades and thousands of students. Some classes have had pass rates as high as 100 percent, some lower than 75 percent, but overall the rate has stabilized at around 85 percent. Keep in mind that people who are able test takers normally do not use my services. My guess is that the average person has failed the PRAXIS three to five times before coming to me.

The following letter came to me from a successful PRAXIS student in South Carolina:

To Dr. Charles Hatch and the CWH Staff:

I wanted to send a letter of appreciation for all of the miraculous and marvelous assistance your services have been to me. I have been on the teaching journey for quite some time, and there has been no doubt that it is the profession for me. However, through many unsuccessful attempts at PRAXIS I, the Reading Portion in particular, I often times wanted to surrender the dream to be a teacher. I had come to a point in life where I was seriously considering other options in life (not trying anymore to pass the test to go on to pursue teaching). Then, I was reminded of the tremendous results that came from

CWH. Hope is all I had by the time I made the call. After much hard work and Dr. Hatch's determination and belief in my abilities, I passed the Reading Portion of PRAXIS I.

Then, PRAXIS II awaited, and as an English major, this would require three different tests to complete. I came, once again, with hope to Dr. Hatch. He, yet again, challenged me to do my best. He had me sign up for all three tests to be taken on the same day. I was afraid, but after we worked hard in preparing for the tests, I was ELATED to call him and tell him the good news . . . I had passed all THREE!! Words sincerely cannot express that day that I opened the scores. Dr. Hatch told me I did not believe in my abilities enough, and that if I started believing more, I would surprise myself every time.

Thanks from the bottom of my heart. It is now the day before August 1st. School starts in 21 days. I have been working hard in my classroom preparing for the students I have been dreaming of for so long. My dream seemed so far away, but because of God's greatness and blessing me with Dr. Hatch and CWH, my dream is only days away from being 100% official!

God bless you all,
[Student Name]
English Teacher
July 31, 2007 (Reprinted with permission from the student)

By 1990 I had expanded the NTE workshops from South Carolina to include the Southeast, where I have conducted workshops from Louisiana to Maryland and Pennsylvania.

A second expansion also took place. A broader array of preparations was offered. Schools and individuals asked for help with ACT, SAT, LSAT, and GRE tests.

I have discussed my experience because it is on the basis of this work that I have developed my preparation approach.

REFERENCES

Bobrow, J. 1985. *Cliffs math review for standardized tests*. New York: Wiley.

Covino, W. A., and Orton, P. Z. 1986. *Cliffs verbal review for standardized tests*. New York: Wiley.

Hawkes, B., ed. 1999. *Guide to standardized test preparation*. Upper Saddle River, NJ: Globe Fearon.

Powers, D. E., and Rock, D. A. 1998. Effect of coaching on SAT I: Reasoning scores. College Board Report 98-6. Princeton, NJ: College Board.

Laying the Foundation

ATTITUDINAL FACTORS

Successful test preparation is always based on the presence of certain attitudinal factors. The participant or student must be focused on improvement and desire to perform well. Without this, nothing else can happen. Stated in negative terms, you cannot force someone to pay attention, to want to improve, or to dedicate constructive time to preparation.

Unfortunately, over the years I have had both groups and individuals who fit this negative characterization. I recall a group of college students in an education program who had the greatest problems passing PRAXIS I in reading, writing, and math. They were being paid stipends to become teachers, and as a result were paid and required to attend my workshop. However, they did not want to be there. They resented the time the class took, and they refused to cooperate in any significant way. One student even refused to turn off his iPod or put away his headphones. He wanted to make sure I knew he was not going to listen or participate. The program director even told me when I began the first five-hour session not to give any breaks because the students would not return! He really knew those fellows. If I started a class with twenty, there would only be a half dozen present at the end. They also failed to improve to pass the test. Small wonder!

Individuals as well as groups can create their own attitude-based failure. I recall a teacher who was brought to my class by her husband, who enrolled her. She wanted no part of the process and, of course, gained nothing.

Recently I taught a workshop for teachers who needed to pass the certification exam. One of the participants referred to herself several times as "slow and dumb." I was careful to talk about this and how destructive such an attitude can be. For both of us to be successful, me as a teacher and her as a student, that attitude needed to be changed. It's like a football team mired in a long losing streak. After you have lost, say, thirty-five games in a row, it is almost impossible to see yourself as successful in any way. A change in attitude is necessary, otherwise both of them, my student and the football team, will continue to fall short of their goal.

I also worked with a student who needed to improve her PRAXIS I reading score in order to advance to the final undergraduate education courses. Her entire career as a teacher rode on this test. She was disappointed because I showed her the ways she needed to work on vocabulary, comprehension, and speed to raise her score. What she really wanted was a painless way for me to get her to pass immediately. She also admitted later that she did not read, did not like to read, and had no desire to change. It is easy to see how the interaction of her attitudes and weaknesses made test score improvement nearly impossible.

In a personal note, a student who had just failed the PRAXIS I reading test told me about her test taking and preparation in the following way:

1. I did not follow the reading.
2. I did not read for meaning.
3. I guessed because the paragraph was too difficult or just confusing.
4. I did not use Type II for finding the correct answer.
5. I really didn't study, because how can you prepare for something that you don't know is going to be on the test. (E-mail correspondence, November 16, 2007)

It is obvious that fundamental change has to take place before she will be able to be successful on this particular test. (For a discussion of the Type II she mentions above, see Chapter 2.)

Theoretically, one of the most important individual characteristics that affects learning is attitude (Gordon et al., 2007). Other related concepts are motivation, cognitive expectations, personality, cognitive styles, and mood. In actuality, these mesh to form successful or unsuccessful test takers.

Attitudes can be so complex that a test preparer cannot make any progress because of a web of conflicts that exceeds remedy. A day care teacher was sent to me by her mother, who ran the day care center and was her daughter's employer. The daughter wanted to pass and knew that she needed to apply herself to make significant gains, but she could not bring herself to do the work just because her mother wanted her to do it. These internal conflicts made it impossible for her to focus on preparing. Her rebellion against her mother was just too strong to allow her to put in the effort to pass.

In 2007 I had another teacher who only needed to pass one more test to become "highly qualified" in Special Education. She came to me for help but was unhappy with the position, disliked the school, and wanted to move away to take a sales job that would double her pay. The bottom line was that failing the test forwarded her "real" goals and even allowed her to move in with her current boyfriend. The dice were loaded against success.

Attitude has always played a significant role in the success of instruction. The research on this aspect of learning is found under several labels: the Pygmalion Effect (also known as the Self-Fulfilling Prophecy) and the Rosenthal Effect. All are related. Pygmalion was the sculptor described by the Roman writer Ovid who fell in love with his own statue of the perfect woman, called Galatea. This idea resurfaced in the writings of George Bernard Shaw, who created the story of Eliza Doolittle, a flower girl who is "transformed" into a lady by Professor Henry Higgins, who instructs her in proper speech, dress, and manners. The story reached even wider audiences as the Broadway musical "My Fair Lady."

In Rosenthal's research, teachers were given incorrect information on the aptitudes of individual students. Those students who were incorrectly identified as potential high achievers were found to make significant academic gains based on the teachers' erroneous expectations. That is, the expectations created different interactions, which in turn resulted in improved performance. These performance-boosting interactions were characterized by more smiling and eye contact (Rosenthal and Jacobson, 1992).

Expectations play a significant role in performance. Recently the *State Newspaper* of Columbia, South Carolina carried the following headline: "Women's Math Skills Linked to Expectations" (2005, p. A14). This article outlined the research of Steven J. Heine at the University of British Columbia. Women who were told that there was a genetic difference that led to men outperforming women in math did in fact show weaker performance than ones who were told that math performance differences were due to differing treatment by teachers and other environmental factors. The higher-performing group, that is, the ones not told that performance was genetically linked, scored nearly twice as high as the others. This study was narrow in that it only included Canadian women studying math, but the principle remains: the Pygmalion Effect is alive and well.

In the arena of motivation, I can recall students telling me about prep classes where the instructor would begin by saying something like, "Anyone who can't pass this test is too dumb to teach." It is hard for me to imagine that many students exposed to this attitude would be motivated to prove the instructor wrong.

Let me conclude on a more positive note. An instructor will find that a motivated group of students focused on improving test performance will be the most energizing group ever encountered. They have kept me teaching for three decades and they motivate me every day. Their letters of success resonate years after being written and in turn motivate others to emulate their success.

HEALTH FACTORS

Certain health concerns need to be presented in any test preparation context. Sometimes (for example, in the case of younger children) the responsibility for improving these areas falls on the instructor or a responsible adult.

Sleep

Getting an adequate amount of sleep has a considerable effect on any person's performance. We can seriously reduce physical and mental abilities by sleep reduction. Certain special circumstances can cause a temporary sleep pattern change. However, the real concern is not to get a good night's sleep before a test, but to get adequate sleep during the weeks and months leading up to the test.

Interesting research with rats at the University of California at Berkeley has relevance to our focus on test preparation. Rats were divided into two groups, those with adequate sleep and those allowed only half as much. The latter group had a much harder time learning a maze, as well as remembering the way to the exit. There even seemed to be marked differences in brain development. The sleep-deprived rats had a harder time growing necessary neurons (termed neurogenesis). The conclusion was that "mild, chronic sleep restriction may have long-term deleterious effects on neural function" (Netscape News, 2006). The same source adds a comment concerning research done at the University of Pennsylvania that eight hours of sleep was the magic number that allowed persons to make only about one-tenth the number of errors, compared to persons with only six hours of sleep. Statistically, persons with the lower sleep level had performance comparable to persons who had not slept for two days.

Dr. Carl Hunt of the National Center on Sleep Disorders lists five consequences of sleep deprivation, all of which have negative consequences for test takers:

1. Attention decreases and reaction time is slowed.

2. Ability to focus on multiple sources of input, such as one would have when solving problems or relating various aspects of a longer written passage, is reduced.

3. Creativity is lowered. The sleep deprived are less likely to produce an adequate number of alternatives, so options for them are reduced and test scores lowered. Imagine a student answering a long essay question. He or she in planning needs to come up with a number of approaches and choose the best. Lowered creativity will lessen the number of options.

4. Memory loss. The sleepless student is simply not able to remember as much as a student with adequate sleep. The former can't marshal enough facts.

5. The sleep-deficient person is unable to operate and process information as quickly as someone with adequate sleep. On a timed test this difference may be critical. (Netscape News, 2007)

Teenagers are especially prone to sleep deprivation, which can result in learning problems, mood swings, and poor health. In fact, falsely diagnosed attention deficit hyperactivity disorder may just be lack of sleep! Teens need at least nine hours of sleep, but some research finds over half of them getting less than seven hours, and a fifth are getting less than five hours (Epstein and Mardon, 2007).

An eye-opening experience has been for me to ask prep students how much sleep they had the previous night. Nearly half will typically tell me they have had less than seven hours, and quite a few say only three or four! I have always tried to encourage my students to aim for seven to nine hours of sleep every night. I realize that there are some circumstances where this is just not possible, but regular, adequate sleep is a test preparation necessity.

Nutrition

Sometimes nutritional habits can disrupt sleep patterns. I recall one student who confided to me that she could not get more than two or three hours of sleep each night, but she did not know why. Then she told me that she drank a Dr. Pepper after every class and with meals—six to ten each day! She was addicted to caffeine and had to kick the habit to improve her sleep in order to pass. Situations like this are within the power of a workshop leader to influence. Drinking sodas, diet or regular, is associated with an increased risk of metabolic syndrome (Netscape What's New, 2007). Persons with metabolic syndrome tend to have large waistlines, high blood pressure, high blood sugar, low levels of good cholesterol, and high levels of bad cholesterol (triglycerides). This combination of negative factors naturally leads to increased levels of heart disease. The finding is based on the well-known longitudinal study of the residents of Framingham, Massachusetts. Of course, this does not mean that the sodas cause the negative characteristics; rather, the two appear to be associated.

Schoenthaler et al. (1991) found that a slight degree of malnutrition resulted in intelligence decreases, which in turn lowered academic performance. In a similar vein, the American School Food Service Association (1989) found that fourth graders with the lowest amount of protein in their diets had the lowest academic performance. Anemia can also lead to an array of problems like "shortened attention span, irritability, fatigue and difficulty with concentration" (Parker, 1989). An article in *Scientific American* found that poor prenatal nutrition and/or poor postnatal nutrition resulted in lowered scores across a whole array of academic tests (Brown et al., 1996). It would seem that malnutrition has a strong and understandable effect on the development of brain cells in very young children, who may not exhibit the results for years. Alaimo et al. (2001) documented that elementary-aged children of food-deficient families were more likely to be retained a grade and had lower arithmetic scores than food-sufficient families. The Center on Hunger, Poverty and Nutrition Policy at Tufts University (1995) documented the significant academic losses in children with even mild malnutrition.

Pollitt et al. (1991) reported that missing even one breakfast would measurably retard academic performance in otherwise well-nourished children. A whole array of studies documented the academic improvement resulting from the addition of a school breakfast program (Action for Healthy Kids, 2004).

From Great Britain comes additional research on a nutritional relationship long suspected by parents and professionals alike. The British Food Standards Agency has linked food additives and childhood hyperactivity, attention deficit disorder, and a decrease in attention span. The research conclusion was that children should be exposed to reduced levels of both artificial colors and preservatives (Study Ties Food Additives, Hyperactivity in Children, 2007).

The effects of improved nutrition on achievement should never be ignored.

Exercise

Here again, people know what they should be doing—they just don't do it. One current medical finding is that for a group of nurses, there was clear, measurable improvement in health as the subjects increased their moderate exercise (walking) to 180 minutes per week. After that the improvement was harder to detect, but there was certainly no decline. This leads to the conclusion that in test preparation, an exercise goal should be approximately that figure—180 minutes a week. The basis was an analysis of 72,488 nurses who had varying levels of exercise. The dependent variables were the incidence of nonfatal coronary incidents and Type II diabetes. Of special interest to currently sedentary persons is the fact that beginning exercise had a great effect on the improvement in health. So, it does not seem that a person has to have a long history of sufficient exercise to benefit. It is never too late to start (Manson et al., 1999). It didn't seem to matter how that exercise time was broken down in segments, as long as the total was reached.

The Harvard School of Public Health (2006) enumerates the following benefits of moderate exercise:

1. Improves your chances of living longer and living healthier.
2. Helps protect you from developing heart disease or its precursors, high blood pressure and high cholesterol.
3. Helps protect you from developing certain cancers, including colon and breast cancer.
4. Helps prevent or control Type II diabetes.
5. Helps prevent arthritis and may help relieve pain and stiffness.
6. Helps prevent the insidious loss of bone known as osteoporosis.
7. Reduces the risk of falling among older adults.
8. Relieves symptoms of depression and anxiety and improves mood.
9. Controls weight.

A number of studies support the positive relationship between greater physical activity and higher academic performance (Action for Healthy Kids, 2004).

Lee et al. (2003) conclude that exercise can even be beneficial to persons out of shape, elderly, and/or with disabilities. A group of over 7,000 derived as much benefit from thirty-minute walking sessions as did fit individuals from similar time spent on more strenuous activities.

This finding is further focused by a report from the University of Leipzig, Germany, which found that moderate exercise actually repaired damage to blood vessels and muscles, especially in the heart! With a group of thirty-seven adults, exercise seemed to stimulate the production of stem cells, which did the repairs. There was one caveat—the exercise had to be ongoing, not just a bit here and there (Compuserve, 2007).

Vision

Since most achievement tests are given in written form, the inability to see the test clearly will be a negative factor for some people. Often the person will even be unaware that a problem exists or that it is as severe as it actually is.

Though a simple visual screening may not detect all problems, it is at least a start. However, most of these will not detect problems where they are most critical for a test taker—close vision.

Working with adults, I have found that perhaps 5 percent have an uncorrected vision problem that has a negative effect on test performance.

Sometimes, though it is rare, the problem can be critical but treatable. Some years ago one of my students, who thought she had no vision problem, had an eye exam upon my urging. The doctor found growths on both eyes that he successfully removed. The student then went on to pass the test that she could now see clearly.

Vitamins

If nutrition plays a part in good test performance, then it is hard to argue against the addition of a multivitamin to a diet. Many persons find that the use of supplements increases energy, attention, and memory, and raises the general level of physical health. Avoiding one bad cold would be a welcome efficiency booster for most people as they prepare for an important test.

Health Behavior Changes

Recent marketing research sheds light on effective ways that test preparers can influence behaviors that earlier seemed to elude change. The work of David Sprott and others has focused on the effect of simply asking subjects a question. He terms this the "question-behavior effect." He finds "that behavior change occurs after the question is asked (as compared to a control group who are not asked the question)" (Sprott et al., 2006) In a related article, Fitzsimons and Williams (2000) wrote, "Results show that individuals asked to report behavioral intent (vs. those not asked) are more likely to choose options that are highly accessible and positively valenced." Further, "This suggests that effect of intent questions on subsequent behavior is primarily the result of automatic as opposed to effortful processing" (p. 195).

The practical effect of the above seems to be that preparation leaders can increase healthful behaviors by simply asking about them while pointing out a desired goal. For example, according to these findings, many students will increase time spent on exercise after being asked how much time they spend while touching on a desired amount. For example, I often ask the following question: "Raise your hands if you regularly get 180 minutes of exercise each week."

TEST ANXIETY

Some people become their own worst enemies by letting excessive test anxiety lower their scores. To some degree, this problem can be solved by careful training and self-hypnosis techniques.

In the early 1980s I was approached by a test taker whose primary problem was test anxiety. She had taken the National Teachers Exam (now called PRAXIS) dozens of times, always failing. Her anxiety had started high and just got worse. Her migraines started on Fridays and dissipated on Sundays of test weekends. Actually, the more often she failed, the higher her anxiety. After I taught her some simple techniques for relaxation that allowed her to reduce the level of anxiety, she passed.

The relationship between anxiety and test performance is complex and not linear. It is actually shaped like an inverted "U," with low performance associated with both high and low anxiety. The optimum scores come with moderate anxiety. Students who are engaged, who care about the result, and who are able to focus do the best.

I have always had an image of a student with low anxiety. I see a junior high student who encounters a standardized test that has no real bearing on course grades. He or she will not be engaged or put forward much effort. I can see that student quickly filling in an answer sheet, making the responses fit a set pattern—say, constructing a Christmas tree on the form. The result is a poor score. In these cases, scores will rise when anxiety is increased; for example, student involvement (anxiety) is raised by adding some positive reward for doing well, such as a pizza party for the whole group if the scores meet a certain standard.

In this area, I feel that there is a clear difference between children and adults. A common problem with adults, especially women, is excessive test anxiety. On the other hand, a common problem with younger test takers is low anxiety. This explains the success of programs that raise children's anxiety (or concentration, which is closely related) with rewards for good test performance.

To summarize, the problem with anxiety is to find ways to lower the level for persons on the high side and raise it for persons on the low side. Since the two ends of the continuum seem to be age related, different approaches would seem to be in order for adults and children.

If you were to ask a typical group of adult test takers whether they were comfortable with their level of anxiety on a given test, almost half would indicate uncomfortable. It is this group that needs and appreciates help.

The comfortable group encompasses people who tend to be more even tempered and who are not as subject to temperament fluctuations. It is encouraging that most are willing and able to tell a workshop leader about their basic test anxiety stance.

REFERENCES

Action for Healthy Kids. 2004. The role of sound nutrition and physical activity in academic achievement. www.actionforhealthykids.org (accessed August 18, 2006).

Alaimo, K. et al. 2001. Food insufficiency and American school-aged children's cognitive, academic and psychosocial development. *Pediatrics*, 108(1), 44–53.

American School Food Service Association. 1989. Impact of hunger and malnutrition on school achievement. *School Board Food Service Research Review*, 1(Spring), 17–20.

Brown, L. et al. 1996. Malnutrition, poverty and intellectual development. *Scientific American*, 274(2), 38–43.

Center on Hunger, Poverty and Nutrition Policy. 1995. Statement on the link between nutrition and cognitive development in children. Medford, MA: Tufts University.

Compuserve. 2007. Read this: You'll start exercising today. What's New, www.compuserve.com (accessed September 7, 2007).

Epstein, L., and Mardon, S. 2007. Homeroom zombies. *Newsweek,* 150(12), September 17, 64–65.

Fitzsimons, G., and Williams, P. 2000. Asking questions can change choice behavior: Does it do so automatically or effortfully? *Journal of Experimental Psychology: Applied*, 6(3), 195–206.

Gordon, E. E., Morgan, R. R., O'Malley, C. J., and Ponticell, J. 2007. *The tutoring revolution: Applying research for best practices, policy implications, and student achievement.* Lanham, MD: Rowman & Littlefield.

Harvard School of Public Health. 2006. Exercise. www.harvard.edu/nutritionsource/exercise (accessed August 18, 2006).

Lee, I. M. et al. 2003. Relative intensity of physical exercise and risk of coronary heart disease. *Circulation*, 107, 1110–1116.

Manson, J. E. et al. 1999. A prospective study of walking as compared with vigorous exercise in the prevention of coronary heart disease in women. *New England Journal of Medicine*, 341(9), 650–658.

Netscape News. 2006. Uh oh: Dire effect of skimping on sleep. www.netscape.compuserve.com (accessed October 24, 2006).

Netscape News. 2007. Top 5 consequences of too-little sleep. www.netscape.compuserve.com (accessed November 7, 2007).

Netscape What's New. 2007. Diet drinks: Scary warning! www.netscape.compuserve.com (accessed September 2, 2007).

Parker, L. 1989. *The relationship between nutrition and learning: A school employee's guide to information and action.* Washington, DC: National Education Association.

Pollitt, E. et al. 1991. Brief fasting, stress, and cognition in children. *American Journal of Clinical Nutrition*, 34(August), 1526–1533.

Rosenthal, R., and Jacobson, L. 1992. *Pygmalion in the classroom: Teacher expectations and pupils' intellectual development.* New York: Irvington Publishers.

Schoenthaler, S. et al. 1991. Controlled trial of vitamin supplementation: Effects on intelligence and performance. *Personality and Individual Differences*, 12(4), 361.

Sprott, D. E. et al. 2006. The question-behavior effect: What we know and where we go from here. *Social Influence*, 1(2), 128–137.

Study ties food additives, hyperactivity in children. 2007. *State Newspaper* (Columbia, SC), September 7, p. A7.

Women's math skills linked to expectations. 2005. *State Newspaper* (Columbia, SC), October 20, p. A14.

2

Broad Basics

One important aspect of the approach of this book that is quite different from the one usually adopted is the attention paid to broad basic skills and understandings. Too many approaches rely heavily on test item practice and cheerleading. I have found that approach to be both inefficient and unsuccessful.

Most students are able to make serious gains by improving the general skill of reading. A possible exception to this is in higher math, because those tests are less reliant on reading than others. Even here, a serious weakness in word problems may reflect a weakness in reading.

Another way to look at the positive results from reading improvement is to look toward the future of most students—college. A study by the ACT as reported by the Associated Press (Netscape News, 2006) noted that from a sample of 1.2 million students in 2005, only 51 percent were proficient enough in reading to cope with college assignments! Conversely, 49 percent were not. Anything that can be done before high school graduation to make students better readers will be of great benefit in later years. This means the SAT/ACT preparation workshops need to emphasize systematic evaluation of reading performance and follow up with practice and drills to improve speed, comprehension, and vocabulary. It is exactly those activities that many preparation programs do not include. They work solely with practice questions, dubious "pointers," and cheerleading activities.

Another way to look at this issue is from the point of view of cognitive learning theory. One important component of individual differences is availability of language templates. In addition, novice learners are characterized by both a limited knowledge base and limited use of language to code and store information (Gordon et al., 2007).

COMPREHENSION

The first and probably the most important aspect of reading is comprehension.

Too many students read but simply fail to gain a sufficient level of comprehension to respond to a question correctly. They are constantly answering their interpretation of the question rather than the one that the item writer intended.

A few years ago I asked a PRAXIS student to read a short test prompt of about 200 words and summarize. After she read the paragraph, I covered the words and started a discussion. She had virtually no idea what the content was. She thought it might have had something to do with some war, but she was uncertain. When she "read" she simply followed a procedure of decoding words sequentially and never paid much attention to the ideas and how they were interrelated. (It was actually about the 2004 presidential election.) This is poor comprehension. I recall another student who would read a prompt and then read alternative "A," then read the prompt and read alternative "B," then read the prompt, and so on. She had to read the prompt six times! This meant that each time she read there was no comprehension; she was just looking back through to see if there was a match to the choice being considered.

Think of the problem another way. Assume you are responsible for test preparation at any level. You might assume that your primary responsibility is to "cover" or review material with an emphasis on practice items similar to the test. This, by the way, is a format adopted by many SAT/ACT test preparers. However, you pay little or no systematic attention to improving the skill of reading. It is easy to imagine students missing many questions where they have reviewed the material and "know" the answer because they fail to understand the question precisely.

Recently I helped a student prepare for the LSAT exam used for admission to law school. The test uses a number of sections to assess underlying skills considered necessary to study law. Included are reading comprehension, logic, and analysis. Closer examination of the questions reveals that they are generally reading comprehension questions with a heavy load of vocabulary, complex sentences, and complicated concepts. The student had taken the test a number of times, had consistently low scores, and had not been admitted to law school. Because she was not a strong reader, she had trouble. She could do reasonably well on questions that required a literal understanding but had much difficulty with questions that required inference. In short, she knew what it said but had little idea what it meant. The diagnosis lead to a different method of preparation than the one she had tried before, which was characterized by endless analysis of sample questions in a private seminar that cost $1,200 but never really addressed her fundamental weaknesses! She was willing to invest the time and effort to make real improvements in basic reading skills, but some students are not willing to make this kind of serious effort; they want a "quick fix." For the latter a magic pill would be the perfect answer. I remember another student years earlier who reacted to my first class with the remark that I really wanted them to make deep-seated and fundamental changes in lifestyle and approach in order to pass a test. She had gotten it!

In November 2007, a college student wrote me the most amazingly honest and insightful comments on her own reading weaknesses. After failing the PRAXIS I Reading test yet again she wrote me the following self-analysis:

1. I did not follow the reading.
2. I did not read for meaning.
3. I guessed because the paragraph was too difficult or just confusing.
4. I did not use Type II for finding the correct answer. [See below for a discussion of Type II.]
5. I really didn't study, because how can you prepare for something that you don't know is going to be on the test.

This story does have a happy ending because she wrote again after retaking the test in December, and she had passed. I absolutely believe that the five statements above characterize too many students, most of whom do not receive remediation.

Failure to attend to the underlying basics results in a weak preparation program. Improving reading comprehension can happen, but the process is slow and requires considerable effort. This is not something you can do "to" or "for" the student, but only "with" him or her.

SPEED

Since most standardized tests are timed, reading speed is a factor to be considered. I have found that increasing reading speed into the 200–400 words per minute (wpm) range has great benefit. Many of my students have been told again and again to slow down and understand. I find that working toward greater speed has a great beneficial effect because many students have lower comprehension *because* they read slowly. It is not uncommon for me to find students, high school and beyond, reading 100 wpm or less. Almost invariably they have low comprehension at the same time.

The wonderful aspect of increased reading speed is that it is usually accompanied by higher comprehension. This is a clear win-win situation for a student. I can't tell you how many hundreds of my students attribute passing the PRAXIS to increased reading speed and comprehension. The PRAXIS Principles of Learning and Teaching (PLT) test in particular responds well to increased reading speed. That is because test takers must read a long case study and then construct three essay responses in twenty-five minutes. A slow reader simply will not have time to respond adequately to all three questions.

In the context of a timed standardized test, improved speed will give a test taker more time to consider each question. This pondering leads to more accurate responses and even to a greater freedom for drawing diagrams of questions, which will be explained later in the chapter.

GENERAL VOCABULARY

Time spent on vocabulary enhancement is a slow but effective way to raise test scores. Over the past thirty-five years of test preparation, I have gradually increased the emphasis I have placed on vocabulary expansion. This change has resulted in higher scores.

Expanding vocabulary is a tedious activity avoided by most students. However, the benefits are too important to ignore. Explore this yourself. Take some words of moderate difficulty and ask a typical preparation student the meanings. You will be amazed. For some, you can go down whole columns of words without finding a single word with which they are familiar.

For example, I thought that most college or adult students knew the meaning of the word "apathy." It turns out that many do not. Some words, such as "benign," may be familiar to students, and they know that the word is often used in reference to cancer, but they think it is a harmful or very dangerous form of cancer. That is, they know the context of the word but choose the opposite meaning.

To reinforce the importance of vocabulary, I recall not long ago working with a student on a question. We were looking at the choices A–E, and she said C could not be the answer. When I asked why not, she responded, "Because I don't know what that word means." C *was* the correct answer. In a question, if there is one word you do not know, then you are just guessing.

In a 2007 class I had a college graduate come to me for assistance with the PRAXIS I reading test. As one part of her preparation, I asked her to work on expanding her vocabulary as one avenue to increase comprehension. Her first assignment was to learn a short list of SAT words. After she studied the words for two weeks, I gave her an informal quiz on ten of the words. Not one correct answer! Not even for the first word on the list. Whether I measured her unwillingness to learn vocabulary or her inability to learn words, the result was the same: no possibility to improve reading comprehension. I chose to use SAT words for three reasons. First, they are readily available from any number of book publishers. Second, they are on about the right level, not easy but not too difficult. Third, the Educational Testing Service (ETS) produces both the SAT and PRAXIS, so questions could be produced for both tests that have similar vocabulary and structure. Quite a number of standardized test questions are simply vocabulary questions. I recall taking the PRAXIS Middle School Language Arts Test myself and thinking while I was working, "Words, words, words." This was because correctly answering so many of the questions was simply a matter of knowing the key vocabulary word.

THOUGHTS ON PROCEDURES FOR READING DIAGNOSIS

The most effective approach to improving reading comprehension is to give an individual reading test and to discuss the results with each testee. A positive approach, where students are told that the information will aid in developing their reading ability, seems to work best. Since everyone benefits from improved reading speed and comprehension, time spent on this skill is rarely wasted.

Sometimes the problems encountered are so severe that remediation in any reasonable period is unlikely. Two examples will illustrate what I mean. Several years ago I was asked to help a student pass the Early Childhood PRAXIS exam. Both my testing and her classroom performance showed that the candidate could not read in any real sense of the word. She could recall words to some degree but was unable to attach any meaning or obtain any understanding. The second student was a sophomore at a local college who needed the PRAXIS I, which contains separate reading, writing, and math tests. He could barely read (percentiles all below 5). Oral reading for him was impossible. One day, as I was preparing to teach the class, another professor came into my room to inquire more about the workshop and the progress of some of the students he knew. Then he asked me about this particular young man and noted, "He can't read, can he?" It was difficult to believe that a student could complete courses at the college level with his reading ability, yet he had. Extreme examples like these illustrate that some remediation is clearly beyond the scope of a short series of workshops given in a limited (i.e., two months) span of time.

The main benefit of providing individual feedback on reading is that it focuses the attention of the student on the necessity for remediation. If a means of remediation is introduced immediately the results are generally good, but any improvement is a move in the right direction.

NOTES ON CHOOSING A READING TEST

An appropriate reading test will allow considerable specific feedback, be easy to administer, and be appropriate to the students' reading level. For years I used the McGraw-Hill Basic Skills System to measure reading skills of persons in high school and above. It allowed me to give detailed evaluations but only requires about an hour to administer.

To decide on reading tests to consider, please see the following:

Friedman, M. I. et al. 2003. *Educators' handbook on effective testing.* Columbia, SC: Institute for Evidence-Based Decision-Making in Education.
Mental Measurements Yearbook. Various years. Lincoln, NE: Buros Institute.

REMEDIATION

There is no point in providing students with information on reading skills without immediately giving them the means to improve. Back in the 1960s I used those old SRA (Science Research Associates) boxes with the practice cards, which had reading selections and questions graduated in length and difficulty. For years I have successfully used books such as the following:

Schmelzer, R. V. 1992. *Reading and study skills*. Reading Rate Boosters, Book
    Two. Dubuque, IA: Kendall/Hunt.
Schmelzer, R. V., and Christen, M. L. 1996. *Reading and study skills*. [Re-
    vised edition.] Reading Rate Boosters, Book One. Dubuque, IA: Kendall/
    Hunt. (Originally published in 1980.)

The most welcome and effective books seem to provide a high number of timed
reading selections, followed by comprehension questions. Repeated drill and practice done on a regular basis over six to eight weeks will improve skills. Setting
realistic goals with a student and then monitoring progress are good approaches.

ABILITY TO "PICTURE" A TEST

A student came to me a short time ago for help with the PRAXIS tests in Physical Education and PLT. He had an uncommon problem—he could not picture what
was wanted. In fact, on one of the tests he got so confused that he cancelled his
scores!

We started with the Tests at a Glance (TaaGs) for all three. These publications
contain information on the number of questions, content, time restraints, and some
sample questions. The key for the PLT is time management. I got the student to see
the structure of the test: four case studies with three essays each for a total of
twelve essays, followed by twenty-four multiple-choice questions. Then I got him
to see himself allocating 25 minutes to each case study (4 × 25 minutes = 100
minutes) and the remaining twenty minutes to the discrete multiple-choice questions. We did a case study and discussed his answer and how it might be improved.

Next, we went to test 0093, PE: Movement Forms–Video Evaluation. The TaaG
enumerated how the two 30-minute questions would be worded. Then we thought
about how the videos would be shown and repeated. We found possible sources for
information to use on the videos. Finally, he understood what he would encounter
and how he needed to respond.

In his case, he was so thoroughly confused by the proctor's presentation that he
could make no reasonable response. After an hour or so going over the formats, he
was much more relaxed and knew how to visualize the tests and what he needed to
do to be successful. Academically over the years, he had had to put forth more
effort than his classmates, but he was willing to do that in order to be the first in his
family to graduate from college and then coach football, his dream.

GENERAL ADVICE TO TEST TAKERS

Many students need to be reminded that there are some ways to approach a
question that will tend to raise scores. Often a gentle reminder will be enough to get
them back on track with improved test-taking strategies.

First, although it seems obvious, they need to be reminded to answer all of the test questions. The only exception to that rule is in the case of multiple-choice tests that use a correction for guessing. In this case, when a student has no idea of the answer, leaving it blank is a viable alternative that will not lower a score. A correction for guessing means that the testing company subtracts a percentage of the wrong from the right.

Not leaving an answer blank also applies to discussion questions. There is no possibility of credit when there is no answer, so even a weak answer is preferable to none.

Second, I urge my students *not* to change multiple-choice answers. Even though I get some students whose second choice tends to be more accurate than the first, most people give their best choice first. I am always dismayed to ask a group about changing answers and find that they "know" they shouldn't change answers but do it anyway. Sometimes they make two or three changes on the same question! Beside the fact that most people are more likely to choose the correct answer first, an optical test scanner can be confused when it senses incomplete erasures and gives no credit. I often have students who fail PRAXIS by only a few points and change answers quite often. I can see how changing only a couple of answers from correct to incorrect could make all the difference between failing and passing.

A corollary to not changing answers is my advice *not* to go back over a multiple-choice test. The prime motivation in reviewing answers is a readiness to change. Changing tends to have negative consequences, so why go back? Where there is only a downside to an activity, why pursue it?

Third, I stress neatness and legibility. Essay answers need to be neat and readable, with few erasures. A short while ago I was working with a student in Mississippi preparing for the PRAXIS PLT, which contains twelve essay answers. The student gave me a sample answer to evaluate. Its appearance seemed fine but was absolutely indecipherable! The student could not even read it herself.

Another aspect of neatness arises with multiple-choice answers where marks are made weakly or outside the indicated answer spots. For example, I have had a number of students who circled the indicated response instead of darkening it in. In this case, an optical scanner would be completely misled and the score lowered to random answers, because the circles tended to cross answer spaces above and below where intended.

Related to this are multiple-choice questions where more than one response is given—multiple answers. Whenever the scanner senses this, no credit is given. Sometimes students change an answer and simply forget to erase the first choice. Sometimes they slip an answer onto the wrong line, inadvertently giving two answers. A third type is the most common. Here a student reads the question, decides on an answer, starts to mark the choice, changes his or her mind, and indicates another choice. The answer sheet then shows a small mark for the initial choice and a larger, darker mark for the second. Usually the first, smaller answer is the correct answer but the students have "talked" themselves out of the first answer. Probably between 5 and 10 percent of test takers lower their scores by committing one of the above blunders while taking a standardized test. Students can easily avoid lowering their scores through greater attention to these simple details.

SEEING THE STRUCTURES OF A MULTIPLE-CHOICE QUESTION

Virtually all multiple-choice questions have a few simple formats. Not all students are familiar and comfortable with all of them. It is even possible to draw helpful diagrams of questions during a test in order to arrive at an answer. This analytical procedure is of no help if the testee knows nothing about the content of a given question, but it will provide considerable assistance where there is some knowledge, even if incomplete. Since one of the main goals in successful test preparation has to be to have the test takers understand the question better, this technique will be of considerable importance. One of the constant refrains that I hear in letters from my students who have improved their test performance is that they have "finally learned how to read a test question."

Structural Type I-A

This type of multiple-choice question is the least complex structurally and is also the type of question most often written by teachers when creating test questions. This structure has one correct response and three or four incorrect ones depending on the number of alternatives. The typical diagram looks like this:

Correct	Incorrect
——	——
	——
	——
	——

The following example will serve to illustrate.

Question: The square root of 64 is:

A. 7

B. 8

C. 32

D. 16

E. 6

Correct	Incorrect
B	A
	C
	D
	E

Remember, just because I-A questions are not structurally complex, it does not mean that they are low in difficulty. A common mistake that I see is that test takers think all multiple-choice questions are in this format and that their only task for a whole test is to select the single correct answer in each instance. Sadly, this is not true.

A variant of this type is the multi-level question, which may look something like this:

Prompt

I. Details

II. Details

III. Details

Possible answer choices are:

A. I

B. II

C. III

D. I and II

E. II and III

There is *one* correct answer, but the whole process is complicated by an additional step where you must decide on the Roman numeral responses before attempting the actual answers.

When I start talking about these multi-level questions in class, I invariably hear many students groan that they just hate them. This means that they approach them negatively, with no clear strategy. It also means that they miss a disproportionate number of them simply because of the complex format.

I advise "solving" the Roman numeral segment first, then moving to the choices for an answer. I even go so far as to cover the final choices with my hand so that I have to focus on the Roman numbered choices first. It helps me to mark each one of them as "T," "F," or "?" Sometimes these multi-level questions can be answered with incomplete information (i.e., without knowing all of the choices). When I took the PRAXIS myself in 2007, I had to answer many of these multi-level questions. When I looked down at the Roman numeral alternatives of one, I did not clearly see which ones were correct, but I did know one that I was sure was incorrect. Then I went to the final choices where there was only one possibility that did not contain my "incorrect" answer. I marked this on the answer sheet and moved on. I am reasonably certain I found the correct answer. However, the overall conclusion is still clear: a logical process can deal with these complex questions even when you are not completely sure of all the alternatives.

Structural Type I-B

This type of question is the exact opposite of the I-A. That is, the testee's task is to find the single *incorrect* answer. In diagram form, the structure looks like this:

Correct	Incorrect
——	——
——	
——	
——	

The following worked example illustrates this:

Question: All of the following are likely to result from cutting down large areas of tropical rain forest EXCEPT:

A. an increase in the species diversity of the areas

B. an increase in erosion by rivers flowing through the areas

C. an increase in the rate of nutrient loss from the areas

D. an increase in the percentage of carbon dioxide in the air

Correct	Incorrect
B	A
C	
D	

I have had some students who simply refused to believe that it was possible to get credit for an incorrect choice; others will tell you that they are looking for the incorrect response but then revert to finding a "correct" answer because that response pattern has been so ingrained that they are simply unable to modify their conceptual framework. Either answering pattern will result in significantly lower scores.

Another all-too-common mistake that students make when encountering a I-B question is to read "except" as "accept." My experience is that about 5 or 10 percent of students make that deadly mistake, which kills any chance to do well on a test. You can confirm this for yourself by simply asking students to decode the word "except" in a test question. Do not be surprised when you start seeing suggested meanings of "take" or "receive." It would be almost impossible to understand or answer a I-B question correctly, given this working definition. The confusion can be corrected in just a few minutes with a couple of practice questions.

It is common for a standardized test to have about 20 percent of the questions fall into this I-B category. This is a great number of questions to miss because of a failure to understand one word.

Structural Type II: The Continuum

I think this type of question causes the most trouble because the answers do not fall into clearly correct and incorrect categories. Instead, they are placed along a scale. The basic diagram looks like this:

Getting credit for one of these requires knowing that a continuum is being used and then placing the choices along that scale. Here is a worked example:

Question: Which of the following laboratory instruments would be **most appropriate** to use in determining the volume of a large block of wood of unknown density?

A. A metric ruler

B. A triple-beam balance

C. A 200 mL volumetric flask

D. A micrometer

Thus, by using a Type II scale to evaluate the appropriateness of each option, the correct response "A" is found.

I have students start by placing response "A" in the middle of the scale, no matter what it says. Then each of the following alternatives is placed on the scale by comparing it to the alternatives already placed *and* to the labels on the ends of the scale. I also encourage them to draw these diagrams on the test as they go to deal with the questions more successfully.

Though common across many tests, the frequency of the Type II question is often determined by the subject being tested. Subjects such as math and science tend to have fewer questions of this type, while subjects such as reading have more. Often students miss Type II reading questions that ask for the main idea or the "best title." The choices do not fall into right and wrong, but rather lie on a continuum from best to worst. If a student approaches a question of this type looking for the single "correct" answer, confusion may result and getting credit is less likely. Often two or even three choices are quite close in meaning and are difficult to place on the Type II scale without strong reading ability.

A student who knows and has practiced these three types of questions has an advantage because he or she has the ability to sort out answer choices through the application of the diagrams. One student wrote to me after passing her PRAXIS: "I listened to everything you told me, did my practices, studied differently and during the test used the graphs I, II and III" (personal communication, January 14, 2005). Many of my students have passed simply because they learned to deal more effectively with questions after studying the three types. They apply a powerful technique to the test questions during the test because I encourage them to diagram the answers as they go. Surely, this takes more time, but an increased percent correct is a big payoff. Increased reading speed can offset the increased time spent diagramming questions. That is, you can spend time learning to read faster so that those minutes gained can be invested in decoding the meaning of questions and their structures.

Good test takers construct models of test questions in their heads without conscious effort, but poor ones do not. Thus, teaching this technique to the latter will allow them to improve scores significantly.

Sometimes test makers seem to go out of their way to make questions more structurally complex than necessary. One ETS test question has remained with me for years. In this question the phrase "Least likely not to" was used. A Type II question is clearly indicated, but the answer desired is on the "Most likely" side rather than the "Least likely" side. Thus, "Least likely not to" and "Most likely" are equivalent. The diagram would look like this:

Most likely   Least likely

*

Too many test takers misinterpret this question and think that it is asking for the "Least likely" alternative. They then go on to miss the question, not because they don't know the material, but because they have gotten lost in the complex verbiage of the question.

THE ANALOGY QUESTION

Tests often contain analogy questions. There is even one common test, the Miller Analogy Test (MAT), which contains only this type of question. Many students find this type of question especially difficult.

In an analogy question, two primary skills are tested. First, the student must understand how an analogy works, that is, the desired structure of the best answer. I recall working with a student who wanted to improve her score on the MAT. My first question was, "What is the desired relationship between the four words of an analogy?" She did not know that ordering was crucial. She thought in the A:B::C:D format that "A" could be related to "D" if "B" was related to "C." This was a critical misunderstanding because, in analogies, one of the incorrect alternatives often demonstrates the correct relationship but in the wrong order.

If the format is A:B as C:D, then A and C must match, while B and D match. Appreciation of an appropriate format will guide the student toward the desired answer.

Example:

ANODE: CATHODE::

A. rate: speed

B. temperature change: volume change

C. saturated solution: supersaturated solution

D. pressure: contraction

E. oxidation: reduction

Choice E best reflects the relationship of anode and cathode in the correct order. That is, anode and oxidation are related in the same way that cathode and reduction are related.

Second, analogy questions require a strong vocabulary. Determining the relationship often draws on secondary or even tertiary meanings. Complicating this type of question is the fact that there is no word context for a reader. There are often ten words that must be known and understood to make a correct choice. I recall an analogy where one word involved was "crack." This was not a noun used to refer to an opening or an illegal drug, but rather the verb meaning "to decode." In an analogy, if there is one word you do not know, then you are just guessing.

ESSAY QUESTIONS

Many tests utilize an essay format. In fact, test makers like ETS are producing more tests that contain essays only or combine both multiple-choice and essay questions. In 2005 the SAT added an essay section. The previous format had just two parts—verbal and quantitative—producing a possible top score of the fabled 1600 (800 + 800). Now the best score is 2400 (800 + 800 + 800). The test developers are hoping that the new test element will have the trickle-down effect of increasing the emphasis that schools place on composition and handwriting.

Persons who have done poorly on an essay test or on the essay portion of a combination test often come to me for assistance. In November 2007 I began working with a student who had taken the PRAXIS test called Middle School Social Studies. On the three essays, she had scored zero points! For each essay she had written an answer for which no value was given. After I had her write a sample answer, the problem became obvious: her answer did not match the question. She would "talk around" the topic but never actually answer it. If the question asked for two explanatory factors, they were simply not there. The trained graders realized this and granted no points. Students must be trained to read questions carefully and then craft an answer responsive to that question. This is by no means a simple process.

STRATEGY OF "ELIMINATION"

I often hear students tell me that they use or have been instructed to use the elimination technique. Too often this is not well applied or well thought out. When I follow up one of these statements with a few questions, the general weakness of that approach becomes evident. The assumption behind this technique is that questions have a single correct answer (see Type I-A above). While this is often true, it is not universal, and its systematic application leads to disappointing test scores. For example, students tell me they are taught to eliminate wrong answers. What happens in the case of the "EXCEPT" question (Type I-B above) when credit is given for the wrong answer? Similarly, how does this strategy deal with a question where all of the answers are to some degree correct (Type II above)? A main idea question would be a good example of the latter. Here the choices are clearly not one correct response with four choices that are absolutely false, but an array of choices ranging from most correct to least correct. Going with the mind-set that one choice is absolutely correct will hinder any student from dealing efficiently and correctly with standardized tests.

Advocates of and students applying this elimination technique are misleading themselves that they have a viable, useful technique. Any preparation program that advocates this technique is probably also deficient in other serious ways.

REFERENCES

Friedman, M. I., Harwell, D. H., and Schnepel, K. C. 2006. *Effective instruction: A handbook of evidence-based strategies*. Columbia, SC: Institute for Evidence-Based Decision-Making in Education.

Friedman, M. I. et al. 2003. *Educators' handbook on effective testing*. Columbia, SC: Institute for Evidence-Based Decision-Making in Education.

Gordon, E. E., Morgan, R. R., O'Malley, C. J., and Ponticell, J. 2007. *The tutoring revolution: Applying research for best practices, policy implications, and student achievement*. Lanham, MD: Rowman & Littlefield.

Mental Measurements Yearbook. Various years. Lincoln, NE: Buros Institute.

Netscape News. 2006. The no. 1 skill teens need for college. www.netscape.compuserve.com (accessed October 9, 2006).

3

Narrowing the Focus

TEST CONTENT

Test content is probably the most complicated aspect of test preparation—perhaps the most often attempted but the least well done. Every test has content, and descriptions of this content are more or less available. Most test makers will offer content summaries and sample questions. Additionally, there are often secondary sources. SAT and ACT tests both have generated a wealth of preparation materials from independent publishers. An example of an open test maker is the Educational Testing Service, which even operates a Web site that provides an array of free informational materials and sample questions to aid in preparation.

TEST REVIEWS

Preparing students for successful test taking assumes that the preparers understand the test, as well as its strengths and weaknesses. Well-developed independent test reviews are a good starting point. I will use as an example the *Educators' Handbook on Effective Testing* (Friedman et al., 2003), which discusses a wide array of tests from early childhood through the GRE. The discussion format is the same for each individual test. Each includes:

1. Test Author's Purpose
2. Decision-Making Applications
3. Relevant Population
4. Characteristics Described
5. Test Scores Obtained
6. Validity Confirmation

7. Reliability Confirmation

8. Objectivity Conformation

9. Statistical Confirmation

10. Acronym

11. Levels of the Test

12. Number of Test Forms

13. Norm-Referenced?

14. Criterion-Referenced?

15. Other Features

16. Feasibility Considerations

17. Testing Time

18. For Testing Groups? Individuals?

19. Test Administration and Scoring

20. Test Materials and Approximate Cost

21. Adequacy of Test Manuals

22. Excerpts from Other Test Reviews

23. Ordering Information

24. Publisher

25. Author

26. Publication Date

27. Cautions and Comments

28. References (Friedman et al., 2003)

The above test information would allow test preparers to plan activities closely aligned to a particular test. Especially helpful would be item 6 above. Below is printed the validity summary for the SAT. Without reasonable validity there is no reason to administer a test.

Validity Confirmation

Test item validity as relates to individual item development seems satisfactory. The development process is outlined in the technical publications and does include trial use. This accounts for the fact that there are more questions on any SAT than actually count for a score. Each testee is presented with one math and one verbal section that only contain questions in development, which do not count in the score calculation. This provides the publisher with an adequate supply of items at all times. However, test items do not seem to be selected from that pool on the basis of their ability to differentiate between successful and unsuccessful college students, otherwise the tests would have greater predictive ability than is shown by current data.

Test response validity is a much more complex and vexing issue. Since the primary purpose of the SAT is to provide colleges and universities with the means to predict a potential student's academic performance, the main validity concern is the extent to which it provides such data (predictive validity).

The following data refers to students graduating since 1980:

Correlations with Undergraduate GPA

SAT Verbal	.40
SAT Math	.41
Math + Verbal	.36
High school record	.42
Math + Verbal + HSR	.52

(The College Board, 2001b, p. 6)

All of these figures are modest and would not be sufficiently high to justify individual admissions decisions. It seems that the addition of SAT scores to the predictive ability of high school grades gives an increase of only about .10 (.42 to .52). Mathematically this accounts for only about a 9% increase!

Another important validity issue needs to be addressed, namely fallacious validity. There is a common but mistaken belief that the SAT is a measure of the quality of high school instruction. That is, the focus is incorrectly changed from individual student performance to a quality measure of the high school, district, and state. This error is reflected in any number of newspaper articles where the SAT performance of high schools, school districts, and states is compared. Several years ago, North Carolina was reported to have the lowest state mean SAT scores. That led to any number of radio and television programs, press releases, and newspaper articles, all of which incorporated a sound of alarm based on the fallacious assumption that SAT scores were able to measure instructional performance. This validity concern is not meant to reflect negatively on the test publisher but only to draw attention to an incorrect interpretation of SAT scores that is prevalent.

Closely related to the above issues and clearly related to the test name changes is the issue of whether test coaching has any effect. Originally the publisher denied that coaching had any measurable effect on improving scores. Then when data would not support this position, the test name was changed from "aptitude" to "assessment." (Friedman et al., 2003, pp. 91–92)

The following excerpt from the same review of the SAT covers item 27 above.

Cautions and Comments

Taking the SAT is a time-honored tradition among high school upperclassmen. How many, many conversations between high school students and adults begin with an inquiry about this test? The SAT has gone through a great number of changes over the years and the process continues. The last major changes in 1994 included the following:

I. Emphasis on critical reading and reasoning skills

J. Reading material that is accessible and engaging

K. Passages ranging in length from 400 to 850 words

L. Use of double passages with two points of view on the same subject

M. Introductory and contextual information from the reading passages

N. Reading questions that emphasize analytical and evaluative skills

O. Passage-based questions testing vocabulary in context

P. Discrete questions measuring verbal reasoning and vocabulary in context

(The College Board, 2001a, p. 9)

The old familiar antonym question is no longer part of the SAT I. Here is an example of that type of question:

VIRTUE: (A) regret (B) hatred (C) penalty (D) denial (E) depravity
[Answer: E]
(The College Board, 2001a, p. 4)

The reliability and objectivity of the SAT I have never really been in question (though more precise information would be welcomed on reliability). The problem is with validity. Because of its purpose, the test must sink or swim on the basis of its ability to predict college performance. The correlation of SAT scores and undergraduate GPA is only about .40. When combined with high school record, it adds only about .10, bringing the correlation to about .50, which is still weak. The whole complex process of development, preparation, administration, and explanation doesn't justify a gain of only .10 in correlation. The costs for individual students are not considerable, but the expense to high schools is considerable. Often SAT preparation courses are offered or required. In addition, colleges also experience considerable expense for little gain in predictive power. It would seem that the most practical course of action would be to abandon the SAT in favor of currently available information like high school rank or high school grades for the purpose of predicting success. Then the function of the SAT could be limited to a small population that would be using these scores in the pursuit of a National Merit scholarship.

In June 2002, the following changes (to be implemented in March 2005) were announced.

1. A third section will be added to the traditional verbal and quantitative sections. It will include both a handwritten essay and multiple-choice grammar items.
2. The verbal section will be renamed "Critical Reading" and expanded.
3. Analogy questions will be dropped.
4. In the quantitative section there will be two changes:
   a. More questions will be included in the Algebra II content range.
   b. The quantitative comparison items will be dropped. These are the ones that require a comparison of the relative value of mathematical expressions or quantities in "Column A and Column B" format.

Some of the motivation for these changes came from the University of California's (UC) threat to discontinue use of the SAT I as an admission requirement for the whole UC system.

These changes, when and if implemented, will tend to have the following effects:

1. The objectivity of the new section containing the handwritten essay will be lower than the rest of the test.
2. The correspondence of the test items to the content of high school curriculum should increase.
3. With the modifications the test becomes less of a predictor of future academic achievement, as originally intended, and more of a measure of past academic achievement.
4. There will be further movement away from the original concept of the test as a measure of "aptitude," which was the original source of the letter "A" in SAT.

It is not difficult to see how a successful SAT preparation program could be configured. There would be units that would address the following:

Increasing reading speed

Improving reading comprehension

Expanding vocabulary

Increasing geometry understanding

Improving performance on word problems

Reviewing the structures of analogy questions

Surveying the grid for student-supplied math questions

Increasing awareness of critical clue words like "except" (Friedman et al., 2003, pp. 94–96)

Helpful information like the above would assist any educator developing a test preparation plan for students.

TEST BREADTH

Standardized tests tend to be broad in scope. For test takers this breadth is both daunting and discouraging. However, since this cannot be modified, test preparation must mirror this same breadth.

Some school curricula are not nearly as broad as the test that students need to take. Or, just as bad, some curricula allow too much freedom of choice to satisfy a degree requirement. For example, a few years ago I worked with a student preparing to take the PRAXIS test in social studies. This is a teacher certification exam given at or after the senior year in college that covers history, economics, geography, anthropology, sociology, psychology, government, political science, and civics. However, this young woman had focused on sociology within her major of social studies and took many classes in this narrow discipline, greatly neglecting the other areas covered in the test, especially history, which encompassed almost half of the test items. So her course selection, though sufficient for a degree, put her at a severe disadvantage on the test. She had to spend weeks of extraordinarily heavy study on both American history and world history to prepare her for the test she finally passed. Until that refocusing took place, there was no way for her to pass the test.

Other programs require the correct material but teach it so poorly that even though the students have taken the subject, they have in no sense mastered it. Some years ago I worked with a student taking one of the PRAXIS science tests for North Carolina. I asked her for a written explanation of gravity. Pretty basic, I thought. Her response made gravity seem like a kind of glue that stuck your feet to the ground. Needless to say, this level of understanding is not sufficient for the PRAXIS.

I can recall another graduate of a four-year college, an English major who needed to pass the PRAXIS exam to teach that subject. The best discussion or analysis she could give of Keats's "Ode on a Grecian Urn" after reading it was that it had "nice" words. Again, this level of understanding is insufficient to pass the test.

BLOOM'S TAXONOMY AND TEST PREPARATION

Another helpful way of looking into the content of most standardized tests is through the perspective of Bloom's Taxonomy. An understanding of the taxonomy and its ramifications can help students focus their study more productively.

The levels of Bloom's Taxonomy, going from least complex to most complex, are Knowledge, Comprehension, Application, Analysis, Synthesis, and Evaluation. These levels are often thought of as a scale going from the least complex to the most complex, like this:

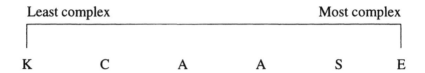

Because most tests consciously focus on assessing student understanding, objective questions are commonly set at the Comprehension or Application levels. Where students often go wrong is in expecting questions to be on the Knowledge level, since that had been sufficient to get them through classes and courses up to that point in their educational careers. I often have students come to me with high grade point averages who do terribly on standardized tests. I believe the possible problem is that when given material they can learn it and give back Knowledge-level answers with great facility, but without ever really understanding. Then when a question is posed that requires understanding, they fail because they have little experience in learning at that level.

An illustrative example from social studies may help.

Sample Question: During a recession, an appropriate fiscal policy would be

A. an increase in taxes

B. an increase in government spending

C. a decrease in the reserve requirement

D. a decrease in the discount rate

From the previous chapter, it is obvious that the question is a Type I-A, with one correct answer and three incorrect ones. The first term that catches the eye is "fiscal policy." Since that is the result of congressional action in the form of regulation, taxation, tax structure, and transfer payments, our focus is on A and B. The other two options, C and D, fall under the purview of the Federal Reserve System (the Fed) and can be automatically eliminated. Now consider the term "recession" in the stem. This denotes an economic downturn associated with rising unemployment, stagnant or falling gross domestic product, and generally hard economic times.

In this case, the role of the U.S. Congress is to stimulate the economy through B, because A would only tend to make a bad situation even worse. Thus, the answer is B. Here is the diagram:

Correct	Incorrect
B	A
	C
	D

However, to reach this conclusion both vocabulary terms in the prompt needed to be understood: recession and fiscal policy. In addition, it is inferred that the reader also knows monetary policy in order to eliminate two of the choices.

Mathematics is unique among the various subjects. It is unique because after the earliest grades, where the focus is on the "math facts," almost all math is taught at the application level of Bloom. It is exactly this characteristic that attracts some and repels others. Some truly poor math teachers manage to "push down" the subject to the Knowledge level and get students to do well, but these students will continue to do poorly on standardized tests for that same reason. Say students work on fractions, then they have a test on adding fractions, work some more and have a test on subtracting fractions, and so on. They learn a pattern and can follow it faithfully to pass a test. If they are later given a test that has questions on percentages, word problems, geometry, the number line, *and* fractions, the students do poorly because they haven't been given practice on a wide range of math concepts together.

Another way test makers gauge a test taker's level of understanding is to present a table or graph and then ask that a student to interpret it. The only way to prepare is to understand the principles of tables and graphs, and students may have little or no experience doing that.

TEST CONTENT VOCABULARY: WHAT THE WORDS MEAN

As all tests have content, they also have vocabulary. Grammar tests expect students to recognize and correct specific grammar errors. For example, most grammar tests will expect that students deal with subject-verb agreement errors. To do that effectively and accurately, a student needs to comprehend the following vocabulary: subject, verb, number, singular, and plural. That same student may also need to understand person, tense, and conjugation. Without these concepts, the only approach is to decide if an answer "sounds" correct.

In the same vein, math tests have their own vocabulary. For example, area, perimeter, and pi, as well as symbols and formulae.

Thus, students need to learn to develop lists of words, terms, and symbols relevant to a particular test. I recall a success story from one of my preparation classes. I was asked to help a young lady prepare for the PRAXIS test in science. Her primary preparation focus was on vocabulary. She worked on it from two perspectives, general words and specific science words. I supplied the former and she the latter. After passing the test, she wrote me that after her study program she was able to say that there were *no* words on the test that she did not know, none. You will understand the extent of her effort when you realize that she had to collect and learn an extensive science vocabulary that included biology (both zoology and botany), chemistry, physics, geology, astronomy, meteorology, and oceanography! Quite an accomplishment in eight weeks.

KEEPING CURRENT

Test makers are assiduous in making sure that the content of the questions reflects current thought. Often textbooks and courses are not nearly as current as the tests. Thus, the content being taught today may already be out of date. The Educational Testing Service sends most if not all of its questions out to field experts for their professional feedback on whether the concepts and the answer are *currently* correct.

For example, only a few years ago it was generally accepted that stomach ulcers were the result of bad eating habits and/or high-stress work. Treatment included surgery as well as a mild diet with antacids of various types, such as Maalox. However, we now know that ulcers are usually the result of a bacteria and can be treated successfully with antibiotics.

Clearly the "old" answers will no longer be counted as correct. So in fields with rapid change, students are expected to be quite current. On the other hand, subjects like plane geometry have not been subject to much change at all and have been roughly the same for 2,000 years.

REFERENCES

The College Board. 2001a. *A historical perspective on the SAT 1926–2001*. Princeton, NJ: College Board SAT Program.

The College Board. 2001b. *Predicting success in college: SAT studies of classes graduating since 1980*. Princeton, NJ: College Board SAT Program.

Friedman, M. I., Harwell, D. H., and Schnepel, K. C. 2006. *Effective instruction: A handbook of evidence-based strategies*. Columbia, SC: Institute for Evidence-Based Decision-Making in Education.

Friedman, M. I. et al. 2003. *Educators' handbook on effective testing*. Columbia, SC: Institute for Evidence-Based Decision-Making in Education.

4

The Post–High School Student

The students who come to me year after year exhibit many common characteristics. I will attempt to weave them together into a narrative focused on a hypothetical but typical student.

This personable individual has always made acceptable or better grades. She has been active in both high school and college (I say "she" because the great majority of my PRAXIS students are female). The college she chose is not one of the more selective public or private institutions, but one that exercises "open admissions," where anyone who applies is accepted—there are no anxious weeks spent waiting for an acceptance letter.

She has tried several majors but settled on education. Now she is having trouble passing the PRAXIS test for admission to the education program.

Although her course grades are quite good (3.0 or better), her underlying skills are weak. Teachers have tailored their courses so that students who "know" the material without understanding get acceptable grades. In addition, reading and writing expectations are low.

This student comes from a very supportive family that has encouraged her to pursue an education that is well above their own. They do not understand why she is having so much trouble passing the admission test. They feel that the college is partially to blame for implementing a requirement for which they give so little assistance.

However, the institution itself has taken certain steps to exacerbate the problem. Since there are so many students having trouble with the test, the school allows them to take absolutely as many courses as possible before refusing to allow registration in the last one or two of the senior year. This lenient policy allows classes to fill up, tuition to be paid, professors to be retained, and programs to be maintained. All of this operates to the ultimate detriment of the student. She comes up to that last year or semester and can't go on, can't graduate, and can't be certified. Both the student and parents like this policy until the crunch comes late in her college career, when changes in major are more costly in both time and money because additional semesters are often required. It seems that often we assist in making decisions most harmful to ourselves. This situation reminds me of persons at a car dealership who are easily persuaded by the salesman to purchase the car they really "deserve." They love it, they enjoy it, and they show it off, but the payments are impossibly high. The eventual repossession compromises their credit. The "helpful" salesman was really no help at all.

Early implementation of the passing requirement would be in the best interest of the student because that would force a change of plans after about two years instead of after three and a half.

Returning to this student, she is academically weak in spite of good grades. Such basics as reading speed, reading comprehension, vocabulary, writing proficiency, and math ability are all relatively low. If tested, most would be below the 20th percentile.

To illustrate this further, I recall a college graduate who came to me for help with the PRAXIS test 0014, called Elementary Education, Content Knowledge. After taking the test numerous times and failing, she decided she needed assistance. This test covers the material taught through sixth grade, not how to teach it. This means that the student, even though she had graduated from high school and college, had not mastered reading, science, social studies, and math at the sixth grade level! Hard to imagine, but true. This level of performance gives severe problems on a norm-referenced test, where passing is set somewhere near the 50th percentile.

The typical student also has a very casual attitude toward health. She is not often able to say that the following minimal conditions are met:

Adequate sleep

Good nutrition

Sufficient exercise

This person will often say she gets only about five or six hours of sleep a night. Inadequate nutritional habits are characterized by an excessive number of sodas, too much fried food, and few fruits or vegetables, coupled with little or no exercise.

She tends not to read by choice and only does required assignments. She tends not to be curious and pursue subjects on her own. She avoids math as well as any "reading" course. In this regard, I remember a wonderful student who did not fit into this mold because she had a wonderful, rich vocabulary. Later she told me that she would often just read the dictionary when she was bored. It is just this kind of curiosity that I admire and is just the attitude I love to see modeled by teachers of my children and grandchildren.

In December 2006, a student came to me for assistance in improving her reading to pass a required test for admission to higher-level teaching courses. She and her parents wanted her to improve. Her father was a voracious reader and had provided her a wonderful example. However, the daughter could not imagine reading a book for pleasure, even if it would strengthen a skill necessary for her to pursue a career. Success was not likely, and that might have been a good thing. I think her presence as a first grade teacher, her goal, would be undesirable.

Crafting a program to enable a student like the one in this example to pass requires considerable effort on the part of both the instructor and the student. If they both realize from the beginning that the process is not simple, quick, or easy, then success may be theirs.

PROBLEMATIC COLLEGE PROGRAMS

Sometimes the educational process in higher education is flawed. Weak students are admitted and retained even though they may never be certified. State regulations can usually be manipulated to maintain class enrollments and thus institutional revenue. One North Carolina institution found that they virtually solved their testing woes by limiting enrollment into their education program to students with SATs of over 1100.

Some institutions are not as current as is needed. Their students learn obsolete material. I remember a colleague who said that he had not read a journal in ten years! This meant that his students at graduation were ten years behind other test takers. Their test performance was certainly lowered because of this.

An important area where colleges and universities can improve test performance (PRAXIS, GRE, LSAT, etc.) is by increasing the match between course offerings and test descriptors. I recently spoke with a student inquiring about how to pass the Speech Language Pathology test for national certification. We discussed how that test has two areas of concentration (educational and clinical) but that many programs do not focus on both. This means that graduates of those institutions will do well on one part but poorly on the other. She agreed that this was probably the problem because her training was largely educational and not clinical.

Another young woman who came to me some years ago was having trouble with the PRAXIS in social studies, which covers history, economics, geography, political science, psychology, sociology, anthropology, and civics. Talk about a broad test—that certainly qualifies. This student (with her college's consent) had concentrated her courses in sociology to the virtual exclusion of the other disciplines. This focus might have worked had she chosen history, but sociology just didn't cover enough of the test content to allow her to pass. Passing continued to escape her until she made a massive effort to gain mastery of the other social studies subjects. She put in an impressive amount of time on history because that represented more questions on the test than any other discipline. She achieved her goal after six weeks of studying nearly forty hours a week! However, the real problem was that the college program *permitted* her flawed and ill-balanced choice of courses. Giving students a wider choice of courses may seem commendable, but not at the expense of failing a test necessary for a person to pursue a career.

Some schools do not come to grips with skill deficiencies, but simply work around them. Students proceed toward graduation and finish, but the problems remain. Several months ago a mature woman came to me because of problems with the LSAT. She had started with a law firm as a clerk, completed a four-year degree, and continued working as a clerk in the same firm for over twenty years. She finally decided to go back to law school but did so poorly on the LSAT that admission was denied. After a day of tutoring with me, I concluded that her reading ability (both speed and comprehension) was the main cause of the problem. Those long, involved, complex questions were above her ability to comprehend. She would go through the test looking for short questions to answer. A solution is possible but will require considerable work and time.

Often another kind of problem is evidenced. A short while ago, during the winter of 2006, I was working with a college student preparing for the PRAXIS I test in reading. She had just finished an upper-level class in tests and measurement the day before. She told me the instructor had conducted the entire class using PowerPoint presentations that he would read and the students would copy. She had finished the class and passed. She had no idea what reliability, validity, or objectivity were. Furthermore, she had no concept of percentile. The college had offered a course that satisfied a state requirement and had the students spend a semester in a class that had no instructional value at all. I think the parents are the real losers in cases like this. They have saved and sacrificed to send a child to college but receive no benefit in return. It may even fit the definition of fraud. No wonder students from that college have a great deal of trouble with the PRAXIS.

ANALYSIS OF WEAKNESSES

A productive focus for a student who has taken a test before is the old score report. From this analysis, broad priorities can often be discovered. This information can serve to guide the subsequent study effort to make it more efficient. Here is an example drawn from an actual PRAXIS test report (0061 Secondary Math).

Content	Number Correct	Number of Questions	Average Performance Range	Percent Correct
Algebra Number Theory	1	8	3–5	13%
Measurement Geometry, Trigonometry	3	12	4–8	25%
Functions Calculus	3	14	4–9	21%

Content	Number Correct	Number of Questions	Average Performance Range	Percent Correct
Data Analysis Statistics, Probability	5	8	4–6	63%
Matrix Algebra, Discrete Math	1	8	3–6	13%
Totals	13	50	18–34	26%

The last column is calculated from the first two. I divided the number correct by the number of questions. The bottom row is the sum of the numbers above. The Educational Testing Service supplies all the numbers except the last column and the bottom row.

Now let us look at what it means. The first and last content areas are the weakest, with only 13 percent correct. These will need a great deal of work and time. The second and third content areas also need extensive attention because they are 21 percent and 25 percent, respectively. The single area that does not need much attention is the fourth content area, with 63 percent correct. To pass most PRAXIS tests, the overall percent correct needs to be about 60. Here we have merely 26, so that will need to more than double!

The average performance range, column four, shows where the middle 50 percent of the test takers scored. Of course, 25 percent were above that range and 25 percent were lower. So this test taker fell within that middle group only once, on Data Analysis.

Another way to look at a multiple-choice test like this is from the point of view of chance. That is, what percent would have been marked correct by chance, if the test taker knew nothing of the subject? Since these questions had five options, chance would have given about 20 percent correct. So this test taker only answered about three more questions correctly than pure chance would have predicted! Preparation here would be daunting because there are serious deficits in four of the five content areas of the test.

Thus, a previous test report can provide a great deal of information to guide study, if properly viewed.

TYPICAL POST–HIGH SCHOOL PREPARATION PROGRAMS

Typical post–high school preparation programs are composed of three day-long classes.

First Day

The initial step begins before the first student enters the class. That step is making sure the participants have a stake in the process. It is usually not enough for them to need to improve a score. Unfortunately, the best motivator is money. The least successful programs I have done have always been in locations where the institution (school or school district) paid the entire cost and in turn required the persons to attend. This approach seems to foster a spirit of rebellion in many people. They seem to say to themselves, "They can make me come, but they can't make me pay attention or do the work required." Remember that student in Chapter 1 who arrived with his iPod and headphones, just to make sure I knew that he was not planning to pay any attention to my workshop. He was one of the students who was actually *paid* to attend my workshop!

A second step also precedes the first session, and that is scheduling. I prefer long classes, usually five to six hours in length. The long classes allow instructor and students to settle in with fewer transitions, such as you might have with five classes of one hour each. The two would not be nearly equivalent because in a single long class more time would be devoted to instruction and less time to transitions (see Friedman et al., 2006). A long lead time between the first class and the test allows serious remediation to take place. It is simply not possible to modify reading speed, comprehension, vocabulary, or serious content knowledge deficits in a few days.

I start the first session easily and even gently so we can all get used to each other. This relieves tension considerably. Too many persons come to me as a last resort before losing a position or dropping out of school. They also come to me after repeated failures on a specific test. I suppose three to five failures would be typical, and fifteen to twenty not rare (my record was one teacher who had failed her exam fifty times; she passed on the fifty-first attempt, after attending my class). As a further calming feature, I read letters from students who have passed after taking the class. Some letters are humorous, some cryptic, and some extensive. My students usually react with relief to discover that others have survived the challenge with success. They will often tell me that a particular letter sounded exactly like their situation.

Next, I start talking about the various parts of the test—how they are graded and what a particular state requires. We go over a typical score report. This allows them to start reading their own test results with greater understanding; later this increased understanding will help to improve their ability to apply prescriptive strategies to their own specific weaknesses.

Each student is supplied with an extensive resource notebook, which is supplemented by materials keyed to a particular test. These test-specific materials are a composite of materials I have prepared, along with test resources from the test publisher. Both help.

Next, I give a detailed overview of the preparation that I term "To Pass." This outlines all of the various aspects that I emphasize.

The first topic that I always cover is health. Within this category I discuss sleep, nutrition, and exercise. Under sleep, I actually go around the room and ask how many hours of sleep each student got the night before. What a revelation! I hear anything from three to ten hours. We discuss. My emphasis is that without regular, adequate sleep, a person's score is depressed.

Next comes nutrition, another eye-opener. I simply ask what each had for breakfast. The answers are an education in themselves. A third of them will say nothing, or its equivalent (just coffee). You will hear the most unexpected food items—pizza, crawfish, goldfish crackers. My emphasis is on getting eating habits back on track. Students know what constitutes good nutrition; they just have to put that information into practice.

Now comes exercise. Too many get none at all. We discuss this, and how simple it is to add a few walks to a week's schedule. Expense need be nothing—no equipment or memberships needed. I encourage them to get at least 150–180 minutes each week, based on research findings.

Now we discuss vitamins. Most don't take them; some have a bottle but don't take them regularly. I suggest regular use of these supplements. This usage is not to take the place of good nutrition, but just to add a measure of insurance to a diet. If taking vitamins regularly lets you avoid one bad cold or illness a year and increases your ability to learn and concentrate, then they are worthwhile.

Finally, we discuss the importance of vision. Several in every class admit that they have been putting off getting checked or updating an eyeglass prescription. This amounts to fine-tuning, but some people really benefit from vision improvement. Many students have written to me after passing to say that correcting a vision problem was an important factor in their getting the score needed.

Usually my next topic is test anxiety. Does that ever get results! Nearly half the students in each class feel uncomfortable with their high level of anxiety when taking a standardized test. I assure them that we will work on that later, when I show them how to exercise a level of control so that they can ratchet down excessive levels of anxiety. A moderate level is fine, but high levels interfere seriously with performance.

This leads me right into talking about generalized test-taking strategies. These are approaches that lead to higher scores if utilized. I first emphasize that successful test takers answer all of the questions. This may only be making a guess, but it is still giving an answer. A natural corollary to this is time management. If a student answers most questions correctly but slowly and leaves a significant number unanswered, failure may be the result. I have discussed test results with many students and I have seen low performance because of time factors. When queried, many reply that they didn't have time to finish. Just as in football, successful test takers need to implement a good game plan in taking a test. This involves managing time so that they have the opportunity to consider each question.

Sometimes I am asked whether test takers should answer each question in order or skip around. I urge them to answer in order. Sometimes students will skip around. This means that they are reading a question not to answer it, but to decide *whether* to answer it. That is a very different process. Focusing on a question and then answering it will give the best results. Also, if students skip around, managing time is more difficult. It is hard to tell when you have answered half of the questions if the answers are scattered. That jumping-around process may also result in recording errors where the answer is marked in the wrong spot.

Another common question my students ask is whether to read the questions before the prompt or after. Often test makers will give a graph or a reading segment followed by several related questions. Students want to know whether to read the questions first or last. On this, I have no strong opinion. I realize that for some students reading the question or questions first gives them a necessary focus. I always tell them that I *never* read the questions first and then tell them why. First, I find it distracting to be concentrating on two things, remembering the questions and comprehending the information. I can read and comprehend, and I can answer the questions successfully, but not both at once. In addition, I point out to them that reading the questions first always means that they will have to read each question twice, when once will suffice. This could be a time-wasting process. Finally, I point out that the answers to some questions are nowhere specifically in the passage! For example, if the question concerns an inferred main idea or a "best title for the passage," then the answer is nowhere because it is diffused throughout the whole passage. Answering these questions is not like looking up phone numbers.

Second, we discuss the negative effect of changing answers to multiple-choice questions. Most test takers "know" that changing answers is a poor idea, but they do it anyway. To convince them I present the following data:

Given a typical multiple-choice question with five alternatives, where A is the correct response, answer changing will fall into three categories.

1. Incorrect to Correct: 4 changes (B to A, C to A, etc.)

2. Correct to Incorrect: 4 changes (A to B, A to C, etc.)

3. Incorrect to Incorrect: 12 changes (B to C, B to D, etc.)

This results in 4 chances in 20, or 20 percent when changing an answer will improve a score, and 16 in 20, or 80 percent, that the score will remain the same or decrease—not very good odds.

Neatness of presentation comes third. Students often forget to think of the grader when writing essay answers. I even suggest that they use erasable ink pens for the essays. These give the formality of ink coupled with an ease of correction that rivals pencil. I hate reading answers with many cross-outs and inserted thoughts that crawl out of a paragraph and meander up the side of a page. If students are given encouragement and practice, they can produce reasonably neat essays. I even give feedback on margins and handwriting.

I also mention how lack of neatness in answering a multiple-choice question can "fool" a scanner. For example, if the test taker fails to erase one answer completely when making a change, the scanner will detect two answers and give no credit. It is also possible to lose credit on a multiple-choice question by filling in an answer slightly away from the intended spot. I think this can happen when a student decides on an answer and sees where it should go but turns to the next question before completely marking a spot. Another common clerical error is making the mark too light. The scanner is dependent on having a reasonably dark mark with adequate graphite to award credit.

What I call "item analysis" comes next. I don't really mean the topic as covered in a test and measurement course, but rather my practical take on how to look into a test question to see its inner structure. To assess a student's initial ability to see structure, I ask a simple question. "What does the word 'except' mean in a test question?" Then I walk around to see the answers they wrote. There will usually be a couple of correct or nearly correct responses in a class of thirty. Many are irrelevant and some are wildly wrong. Some will tell me that it means to take! They confuse "except" and "accept." Can you just imagine how confusing it would be to try to decode a question making that mistake? There would be little possibility of getting credit in that case. Mistakes like that must be corrected before there is any hope of raising a person's test score. I assure my students that we will spend more time on this and related concepts.

Reading comes next. There is probably no topic of greater concern than reading because there is no single aspect of test preparation that is more important to more people. We discuss three aspects of reading that are relevant to test score enhancement. The first is comprehension. All will agree that this must be present; we also agree that *everyone*, no matter how good a reader, can benefit from increased comprehension. We then think together about the two broad aspects of comprehension—literal and inferential—and what each means. The second important aspect of reading is speed. We discuss how many words per minute (wpm) are necessary for a timed standardized test. I posit the number 300. Students usually feel that obtaining that number is an impossibility, but I keep the pressure on to do that and more. The last aspect of reading that we discuss is general vocabulary. We talk about how a weak vocabulary results in excessive errors, which leads to lower scores.

The next topic, content, is another of great concern. Most people who come to me expect that I will spend all of my time going over content, but I don't. My time is better spent guiding them as they expand their own content knowledge. I do go over some things relevant to many tests (more about that later).

Under this content umbrella, we discuss three aspects of gaining adequate information in a content area. The first topic is the comprehensive nature of these tests. Most standardized tests cover more material than we are comfortable answering. A perfect example are the PRAXIS social studies tests, which cover the broad range of history. This means *all* history—all periods, all continents, and all countries! It is a daunting task to be prepared adequately for such a broad test. Also on the same test are questions on sociology, anthropology, psychology, geography, political science, economics, government, and civics. Published test summaries and test descriptors do help and can be obtained from most reputable test publishers. For example, there is a free Test at a Glance (TaaG) for each of the PRAXIS tests published by the Educational Testing Service. In my workshops we use these extensively as we plan a study program for each person. Obtaining a test descriptor is absolutely necessary as a starting point in successful test preparation.

As I recently prepared myself to take the PRAXIS in a field (Middle-School Language Arts, test number 0049) that I had not taught for thirty years, I started with the test descriptor and some sample questions in the TaaG. From these I developed the following list of words and terms that became the basis of my entire six-week study/review program.

Language Arts Review (test 0049)

Metonymy

Synecdoche

Metaphor

Simile

Voice

Narrative point of view

Tone/attitude

Style

Setting

Diction

Mood

Allusion

Irony

Clichés

Analogy

Hyperbole

Personification

Alliteration

Foreshadowing

Euphemism

Jargon

Idiom

Connotation

Denotation

Morphemes

Phonemes

Aphorisms

Anaphora

Person (first, second, third)

Theme

Subject

Elements of writing

   Pre-writing

   Drafting

   Revising

   Editing

   Publishing

   Evaluating

Holistic scoring

Scoring rubrics

Rhetoric

   Purpose

   Types of discourse

   Narrative

   Persuasive

   Informative

Writing style

   Audience

Type of writing

   Expository

   Narrative

   Argumentative

   Descriptive

Punctuation

Word choice

Sentence construction

Overall presentation

This content summary became the basis of my review, which took perhaps twenty hours over a number of weeks. My score of 199 of a possible 200 supports this technique, which keeps the content review closely focused on the published test content.

The next aspect that we discuss is that of being current in the field. Responsible test publishers strive to keep their tests current. However, the test item development process gives clear limits on exactly how current items may be. Usually a publisher can stay as current as a year or two from the test administration date. The problem for test takers is often that they are not as current as the test they are taking, for two reasons:

1. Sometimes the training they received was years ago (twenty years is not uncommon).

2. Some test takers have the handicap that although their training was not long ago, it was not current when they received it. Professors who lecture from the same notes they have used for twenty-five years contribute to the problem. Because *they* are not current, their students in turn have little hope of being current.

On the other hand, I recall a professor honored for the excellence of his teaching who did a daring thing. When he completed a lecture, he dropped his notes in the trash. This forced him to rethink every topic every semester or year to stay abreast of changes.

The last topic we discuss related to content information is vocabulary. I have found that it is impossible to overemphasize the role an adequate subject matter vocabulary plays in passing a test. I can scarcely imagine how a student could spend too much time developing an adequate subject vocabulary. Think of typical test questions. Time and again, answering a question correctly revolves around having a good grasp of the words and terms used.

Finally, I get to my miscellaneous category of areas that are related to many different tests. Here I mention the ability to understand tables and graphs, Bloom's Taxonomy (discussed in Chapter 3 of this volume), and Piaget's theory, which may appear on a number of PRAXIS tests. (Piaget focuses on cognitive development from birth to maturity in four successive stages: sensorimotor, preoperational, concrete operations, and formal operation. Quite a number of questions reference the theory by name, while others expect the test taker to apply the theory to select the correct answer.)

I also note that we will discuss educational measurement and statistics. Last, I mention taking time to practice answering sample questions. Over the years I have gradually done less of this because other activities are more effective in raising scores.

Students expect that most of the preparation time will be spent on answering questions and then going over an explanation of the answers. Years ago I did more of this than I do now. I changed my approach for the following reasons. First, if you can read a question, it probably won't be on a test. Good test makers release questions but do not reuse them. Second, it is hard to learn for an array of randomly presented questions. To learn you have to drop back to an organized, systematic presentation. Most sets of questions or sample tests are neither organized nor systematic. That being said, you can get the feel for areas of weakness by answering questions. That information must be followed not by more questions, but by a systematic study of that material. If you tend to miss questions on the American Civil War, the solution lies in studying the period, not in doing more questions.

I suppose one of my students from Goose Creek, South Carolina, was most important in reorienting my approach. I gave her a book with thousands of sample elementary education questions. She worked hard, memorized each one, and then failed the test because she had not learned or understood the material behind the questions.

You may omit this next step, where I sign a contract with each student. This outlines my responsibilities as well as those of the student. In this, I strive to be as specific as possible. I ask students to commit to twelve hours of study per week and to take twelve pages of notes during that time.

The next item on our typical agenda is an extensive reading test that requires a little more than an hour to administer but gives excellent information to guide each student in remediating weaknesses to enhance test performance. I currently use the McGraw-Hill Basic Skills System reading test, which gives information on a student's reading speed and comprehension. The latter is broken down into component categories, such as main idea and detail. I stress again to the class that everyone benefits from improved reading and that I will accept responsibility to provide appropriate materials for reading improvement and to guide each in their use.

Notebooks come next. Here we walk through the various parts, comment, and make notations, and I show them how I want them to take notes. In the back are recording pages for the documentation of study time. My usual expectation is that students spend twelve hours each week studying material for test preparation. I arrived at this number many years ago and have stayed with it for decades. It is a reasonable compromise between the necessities of preparation and the busy lives my students lead. One of the lessons for instruction derived from mastery learning theory, personal systems of instruction, and cognitive science models is that time actually engaged is important (Friedman et al., 2006; Gordon et al., 2007). We walk through the various aspects of marshalling information to broaden content knowledge.

Because computers and Internet access are now so common, I walk through some Web sites that provide aid for particular tests. At this time I also distribute the test-specific materials that I have prepared.

Now comes a bit of a shock. All students had easily agreed that a broad general vocabulary was a necessary part of test preparation. Now I give them a list of words to be learned for the second class. This assignment provides students a good start on a study regime. Students can start immediately and use initial study periods to good advantage while gathering more specific books and articles. I ask the class members to decide on how many words to include on the first preliminary test.

This is followed by about thirty minutes of working with sample questions. Students answer questions while simultaneously looking for words, terms, and names that they don't know well for a vocabulary list. When they correct their work, they calculate the percent correct to serve as a rough estimate of their subject mastery. We use 60 percent correct as the benchmark. Above 60 percent is considered good, but below that means study needs to be doubled. I recall a student who consistently got less than 10 percent of his four-option multiple-choice questions correct. This amounted to less that half of what he should have gotten correct *by chance*. He would have gotten more correct if he had not read the questions. I could only conclude that he was sure in his mind about what he knew, but that he was wrong.

In this vein, there are a number of areas where students are consistently taught incorrect information. For example, I often ask my social studies candidates what the Emancipation Proclamation did. They have almost always given the wrong answer. They tell me that President Lincoln freed the slaves with that proclamation. Not true. The document said it freed the slaves in those parts of the Confederacy not under federal control. Those were precisely the areas where Lincoln's decree could have no effect. In slaveholding areas where he had control, such as Maryland, Kentucky, and Missouri, it did not apply. It also exempted such areas of the Confederacy as New Orleans and Beaufort, South Carolina, which were occupied by federal troops. So, when promulgated on January 1, 1863, the Emancipation Proclamation freed no slaves. This is the level of understanding that the test questions require. This also illustrates an important aspect of most standardized tests: test makers are looking to determine whether the test taker *understands* the material and has not just memorized some information.

Let's return to our typical class. I now ask some students who are taking a test with essay questions to write one for me. To assist them we go over the following reminder:

TO541

We discuss each component.

T = write the title or topic

O = write a simple outline

5 = number of outline elements and number of paragraphs

4 = number of sentences in each paragraph

1 = number of ideas in each paragraph

This formula helps students remember the steps necessary to create a satisfactory essay (Friedman et al., 2006). Writing by formula creates adequate essays but not literature. This approach is also included in a helpful summary of learning theory by Gordon et al. (2007), which they call a metacognitive strategy. I structure my essay feedback with a form (see the Appendix at the end of this book) that gives specific information on a range of writing concerns such as structure, details, development, and grammar.

Friedman et al. (2006) discuss this concept under strategy 15, Utilizing Reminders, where 173 studies support the efficacy of this technique. One example will suffice—the use of the acronym "HOMES" to remember the names of the Great Lakes (Huron, Ontario, Michigan, Erie, and Superior).

Finally, I go through the relaxation technique, which helps the students learn the steps that will enable them to cope with excessive test anxiety. It is actually a self-hypnosis technique where students learn how to relax their bodies and then move their minds to a "relaxing place." It gives them a tool to exercise some control over what has been for many an emotion with no controls.

Before dismissal, I outline the tasks to be completed before the second class:

1. Work on general vocabulary

2. Work on specific subject vocabulary

3. Fill in study sheets week by week

4. Put notes behind corresponding study sheet

5. Access necessary Internet sources

6. Gather other study materials, such as books and journals

7. Practice relaxation

That concludes the first five-hour session.

Second Day

Before the second class, I prepare the reading results for each student. I also note any anomalies in their answers and propose possible solutions. For example, I find that students often let their minds wander as they take a test. I can see this happening on the comprehension section. When their minds wander, the number of correct answers plummets. When the focus returns, the number of correct answers rises. That is, the correct and incorrect answers cluster. I tell the students who do this to be aware of the problem and to fight inattention as soon as it begins.

As I work on the reading tests, I try to learn the names of my students. My goal is to be able to hand back all the reading results without calling names. Do not underestimate the importance of learning names and calling on students by name from the beginning. The effort to learn them is amply repaid with vastly increased participation and satisfaction with the preparation process.

After taking attendance, I usually begin with a review of descriptive statistics, which starts with measures of central tendency (mean, median, and mode) and variability (range and standard deviation). These are followed by a detailed discussion of the normal curve and the associated scales (percentile, stanine, etc.). I also use this lesson as a demonstration of what it actually means to understand concepts. Often students think they have mastered an idea if they can describe it in some way. For example, they may think they are done when they tell me that a mean is an average and that it is calculated by taking the sum of the observations and dividing by the number of observations. I then give them a problem like this:

> The average weight of three boys is 52 pounds. One boy weighs 70 pounds and another weighs 55 pounds. What is the weight of the third boy?

Many find they just can't do it because they do not understand the concepts. Tests most often ask questions by approaching a concept in a way that has not been covered in instruction. In the above question, the student is not just given a few numbers from which to calculate a mean. The "answer," the mean, is given and test takers are expected to be able to work backward from that.

Another concept that seems to create unlimited problems is the Pythagorean Theorem. Many students can tell me that $a^2 + b^2 = c^2$, but they have no idea how or when to use it. They think it is sufficient to be able to recite the formula. One of my main goals is to get students to look inside themselves, to inspect their level of understanding and gradually remediate it with my assistance. It is something we can do together, but I cannot do it to them or for them.

Next, using the preceding review of descriptive statistics as a base, I cover measures of dispersion or variability, which mesh nicely into the next discussion of the normal curve and some of the educational measurements derived from it. We review in detail range, standard deviation, percentiles, stanines, z-scores, and T-scores. It is only now, after I have provided a basis of understanding, that I hand out the reading results from the test given at the first class. My attempt at this point in a class is always to be able to hand these back without calling any names. I try to learn the student names as soon as possible.

The following is a reading score report for a student having considerable trouble in reading. The scores are certainly low, but not untypically low for many post–high school students who come to me for test preparation assistance.

Category	Raw Score	Percentile
Easy Reading	167 wpm	8
Harder Reading	125 wpm	5
Retention	6/20	3

Skim and Scan	6/30	2
Paragraph Comprehension	11/30	6
Total	23/80	1

I also break down the Paragraph Comprehension category for this student in the following way:

Main Idea	2 correct of 5 (weak)
Detail	1 correct of 5 (weak)
Principles and Applications	2 correct of 5 (weak)
Organization and Structure	3 correct of 5 (OK)
Tone, Intent, etc.	0 correct of 5 (very weak)
Study Type	3 correct of 5 (OK)

(Actual results of a PRAXIS I student in Charlotte, North Carolina, summer 2007)

For the person above, reading improvement is a necessary first step to be accomplished before any realistic change can be made in test scores.

At this point I hand out copies of the reading remediation book that I have used for some years: *Reading and Study Skills*, Book One (Schmelzer and Christen, 1996 [1980]). The book has dozens of short reading selections followed by comprehension questions. Students are able to get feedback on their reading speed and comprehension by using the book. Book Two (Schmelzer, 1992) has an additional vocabulary section and more reading drills. I help each student record individual results and set long-term goals. We read two or three selections until the students are comfortable with the procedures—timing themselves, answering the questions, and recording the results correctly. They continue the drills at home by doing several each week.

The next activity is a real change of pace. We discuss the three multiple-choice item formats, how each looks and how it can be diagrammed. This is followed by many worked examples that students explain on the board. I try not to let any errors appear on the board. Some students who start with great uncertainty only master the technique when they stand up at the board and work through an example with my guidance.

For some students, my way of looking into test questions is a revelation. They have been taught or allowed to believe that each question requires that you "find" only a single correct answer. This is not true, as my long discussion in Chapter 2 illustrates. Some can't really grasp that in "EXCEPT" questions, the desired answer is the wrong one! I have even had a few students who never even accepted the concept and thought I must be mistaken.

In my class at Queens University in Charlotte, North Carolina, over the summer of 2007, I was privileged to have a student who really grasped the above item analysis concepts. Her enthusiasm just jumped out during the class as she realized what I was explaining and how it would impact her test-taking strategy. Gaining this single concept raised her score by 20 percent.

Now it is time for further application of the item analysis procedure. We again do some sample test questions for about thirty minutes. If time allows, a second drill is done.

About here, I quiz students on vocabulary chosen at the first class. For each dictated word, they supply a definition and use it in a sentence.

The relaxation technique, based on self-hypnosis, readies the students for the end of class and provides a good "cooling-down" exercise from the high intensity of the previous four hours. Under my guidance, the students first systematically relax the muscles in their bodies. Then they think the words "relax" and "calm and serene" for a couple of minutes. I then ask them to imagine being in a location where they would be perfectly relaxed. Many anxious test takers need to have tools to ratchet down their destructively high levels of anxiety.

At this point I also list activities for the final class. A typical assignment list might look like this:

1. Complete the reading book through page ____; time, read, answer, and record

2. Work on the remaining vocabulary

3. Continue studying content material

4. Record study times on study sheets

5. Review: item types, statistics, and normal curve

6. Practice relaxation technique

7. Next class: date, time, location (if different)

Third Day

The last class is the least pressured and meets just shortly before the test. We go over what the students will need to do before taking the test:

1. What materials to assemble to take to the test center

2. How to manage time during the test

3. When to stop studying

It is about here that I insert a short review of Piaget's theory as well as Bloom's Taxonomy, because there are questions on a number of tests related to both.

Next, I work for perhaps ninety minutes on how to read tables and graphs. I present a pattern for them to follow in decoding a particular table or graph. I start them with the title, then the caption or description, followed by the horizontal and vertical scales and finally the line or bar of relationship. All too often students omit critical steps in their analysis. For example, I am usually able to show how reading the title carefully is often the key to understanding all that follows. These items constitute a very significant portion of many tests, and mastery of a few simple techniques helps many students achieve a higher score. One of my main points in this regard is that test item developers look at tables and graphs analytically, so their questions reflect this same analytical bent. My students do not find it easy to acquire this skill. All too often, they view tables and graphs in an unorganized way, and they skip over critical portions. One particular test, PRAXIS I in math, has a great number of questions based on graphic presentation.

This is followed by the final vocabulary test, a test simulation exercise, and a review of the relaxation technique.

CHECKLIST FOR THE EVALUATION OF A TEST PREPARATION PROGRAM

The following are some of the questions that should be answered by test preparation leaders to assure participants that the program is legitimate, data based, and taught by a professional.

1. Has the instructor taken the test?
2. How was his/her performance?
3. Has the instructor studied published test reviews and evaluations in such standard sources as:
   a. Friedman et al., 2003
   b. Buros *Mental Measurements Yearbooks*
4. How will the course deal with underlying weaknesses in:
   a. Reading comprehension
   b. Reading speed
   c. Vocabulary
5. What insights will be presented for analyzing test questions?
6. Is feedback from former students available?
7. Are the class/study materials from various sources:
   a. Published
   b. Instructor developed
8. To what degree is the instructor available for student questions and assistance?
9. How may students get in touch with the instructor?

    a. Phone

    b. E-mail

    c. Office

10. What percent of class time will be spent on test item simulations? This number should be relatively small, certainly under 50 percent.

11. What is the instructor's background in test theory? Statistics? Educational measurement?

12. Has the instructor prepared students for this test often? For how long? With what success?

REFERENCES

Friedman, M. I., Harwell, D. H., and Schnepel, K. C. 2006. *Effective instruction: A handbook of evidence-based strategies.* Columbia, SC: Institute for Evidence-Based Decision-Making in Education.

Friedman, M. I. et al. 2003. *Educators' handbook on effective testing.* Columbia, SC: Institute for Evidence-Based Decision-Making in Education.

Gordon, E. E., Morgan, R. R., O'Malley, C. J., and Ponticell, J. 2007. *The tutoring revolution: Applying research for best practices, policy implications, and student achievement.* Lanham, MD: Rowman & Littlefield.

Mental Measurements Yearbook. Various years. Lincoln, NE: Buros Institute.

Schmelzer, R. V. 1992. *Reading and study skills.* Reading Rate Boosters, Book Two. Dubuque, IA: Kendall/Hunt.

Schmelzer, R. V., and Christen, M. L. 1996. *Reading and study skills.* [Revised edition.] Reading Rate Boosters, Book One. Dubuque, IA: Kendall/Hunt. (Originally published in 1980.)

5

Grades K–12

The typical K–12 student is much like the post–high school student described in Chapter 4, except that the habits of the younger student are not so deeply ingrained and thus are a bit easier to modify than those of the older student.

A fundamental problem for K–12 students is that they do not naturally turn to the written word for information or enjoyment; there are too many alternatives that vie for their attention. Just think of the hours that students spend with TV, videos, cell phones, and computers. None of these require the application of the skill of reading. You might suppose that using computers would, but in fact it doesn't because all you need is to catch a few words or sentences.

All of the above electronic gear also tends to foster a kind of frenetic, restless movement that induces students to jump from activity to activity without actually sitting down and focusing for hours at a time, as a book requires. Mark Dewalt's fine book *Amish Education in the United States and Canada* (2006) provides wonderful examples of how successful the Amish educational system is with students whose whole environment fosters focus and deliberation, with no disturbances from electronic media.

Because of this lack of reading, many K–12 students are poor readers, lacking both speed and comprehension, and their vocabulary is weak. Because of these weaknesses, a broad program needs to be implemented. Time and encouragement bear fruit.

Quantitative skills may also be weak, but for different reasons. Here the child does not perform very well on content that has been taught.

For years I have noticed an interesting characteristic of high school SAT students who are enrolled in demanding math courses like Algebra III, Trigonometry, and Pre-Calculus. They are likely to miss *arithmetic* questions!

PROBLEMATIC K–12 PROGRAMS

Often the schools and districts with problematic K–12 programs are not located in areas where highly qualified personnel are easy to hire. If a principal has two openings and receives only two applicants, what selective choice is there? Other districts are bedeviled by past personnel decisions. I recall one district whose goal was to find and hire the *least* qualified persons! They did this for two reasons. First, these people came cheap and budgets were kept low. Second, these people did not rock the boat, and any administrative request was accepted. Principals found that less-qualified persons were submissive in ways that better-qualified persons were not—for example, extra duty was accepted and sponsorships were undertaken.

These problematic districts also tend to have teachers and aides who themselves did poorly on standardized tests. It is easy to imagine that teachers transmit their attitudes and skills without consciously meaning to do so. Persons who are good test takers tend to transmit their own complex conceptions of content as well as the overriding generalizations based on extensive reading. I can recall several examples. Not long ago I taught a class in a North Carolina charter school where one student stood out from the rest because of her reading ability. She could read about 1,200 words per minute (wpm) with fine comprehension. I'm sure her teaching of middle school language arts also included a take on reading comprehension that would be impossible for a teacher who read 150 wpm with only modest comprehension. Having teachers of this caliber was also a partial explanation for why this public charter school had a waiting list for admission and virtually no discipline problems!

These districts may also serve as dumping grounds for educators who have experienced serious problems in other districts. I am pessimistic about a district that has many teachers who drive forty or more miles to work. One troubled district I recall had a teacher who fit the above description. It turned out that he was a heavy drinker who brought his "medicine" to work and turned over most of his classes to his middle school students, who planned the lessons and conducted instruction.

Often these problematic schools are characterized by low-time-on-task classrooms. Each class period can be evaluated not only by how long it is (forty-five minutes, fifty-five minutes, etc.) but also by how many of those minutes are spent on instruction. Student achievement drops as instructional time drops (Anderson, 1995). Not long ago I conducted a workshop in a middle school that had the terribly aggravating practice of making announcements all day long. They would call students to the office, announce bus changes, schedule changes, on and on. I felt like pulling the loudspeaker out of the wall. The net effect of each announcement was to remove at least five minutes from instructional time. I was having problems with mature adults who were highly motivated students, so I can only imagine how much worse it would have been with a class of typical middle schoolers.

Sometimes a school or district consistently focuses instruction in a way that decreases comprehension; the policy is to maintain order at the expense of learning. I remember being told as a teacher to give more seatwork and to do fewer exercises that required students to understand and communicate well. I taught junior high language arts and always incorporated extensive essay writing into my lesson plans. I was convinced that students only become better writers by writing. I remember my principal telling me that he did not know why I did that kind of assignment because the time to correct was so heavy.

Years later I was called back to that same school as a consultant to help raise test scores. Student grades were good, the school was orderly, and discipline was under control, but the test scores were too low. After looking at most of the classroom tests, I told the teachers that they were not aiming any of their questions beyond the Knowledge level of Bloom's Taxonomy. The questions did not even *look* as if they required any kind of understanding. If a student is not required to understand material as a regular classroom feature, when a standardized test comes along that does require it, performance will understandably be low.

Too many students who have not mastered material are promoted again and again. Unfortunately, they get to a point where remediation is not really possible. One year I was assigned to teach sophomore English (English II) in summer school. I had some repeaters and some students taking the course for the first time. Among the repeaters was a student who could not really read. He was sure of the one-letter words (I, a) but the others were a blur. He was completely confused by "is," "it," "at," and all the rest. The first time he attempted to read aloud, the game was up. He had passed all the previous years. How? The football coach told me he really needed him that year because he was a good running back, and he asked me to pass him. Where does a student like that go for help? I referred him for special education evaluation, but the parents objected so no solution was found. I expect he eventually dropped out from frustration.

Some administrators also do their part in creating a climate for poor test performance. Sometimes they choose employees who cannot foster excellence. One principal hired only persons who were members of the same Greek sorority! Another simply disappeared each day. After he entered his office in the morning, he took no calls and did not emerge until after the last child left. Other administrators are the opposite—they touch each person each day, both students and staff. They are totally involved in everything going on in the school. I recall a principal like that in Mississippi. She couldn't see me when I first arrived on her campus to conduct a workshop because she was involved with a parent whose child had missed *one* homework assignment. The problem was solved early. This principal's involvement was so complete that not even this small detail escaped her attention! It also shows what can be accomplished when the big problems are solved and attention is given to the small ones. If you are engaged in putting out big fires, you have no time for fire prevention.

Perhaps the best overall solution for a school or district is to implement as many of the twenty-one successful learning strategies as possible from *Effective Instruction* (Friedman et al., 2006). This book and the strategies documented will allow a school to know and implement a broad range of research-based strategies found by experts to improve learning. One example is Utilizing Reminders (strategy 15 in the above book). By this, the authors mean ways to use keys and memory tricks to enhance recall and thus increase performance.

In my work with students to improve essay writing on PRAXIS, I use the following reminder:

TO541

I give them the following associations:

T reminds them to state the title or topic

O reminds them to write a short outline

5 stands for the number of outline elements and number of paragraphs

4 is for the number of sentences in each paragraph

1 keeps them focused on one idea in a paragraph

Thus, I can simply ask them if they have followed TO541 in writing a given essay. When they have, they have made a significant step toward better writing. They can remember TO541 easily.

Even attention to nutrition can pay dividends to a school or district. I recall visiting a district in the Mississippi Delta that provided a wonderful service to its students—fresh fruit. They had servings of fruit twice a day, at noon and before leaving in the afternoon. In a small elementary school of perhaps 400, the cafeteria distributed 800 pounds of fruit each day—grapes, apples, nectarines, plums, and more. I thought this program had a positive effect on parents, students, faculty, and staff. It seemed to refocus everyone on the well-being of students.

INFORMATION AVAILABLE FROM STANDARDIZED TESTING

Most students have to take a number of standardized tests for which a performance record is available. A careful analysis of this record can give teachers a great deal of information to guide them in setting individualized instruction. Table 1 shows a typical score report for a kindergartener, how it can be expanded and interpreted.

In Table 1, one column, "Percent Correct," has been added to increase the amount of information to guide instruction. All of the above indicate a strong student performing above grade level because all of the Grade Equivalent Scores in the last column should be compared to 0.7, the child's actual grade level at testing.

The percentiles tell the same story, where 59 is the lowest. That is, at this child's

Table 1
Sample Elementary School Results

Subtest	Number of Questions	Number Correct	Percent Correct	National Percentile	Stanine	Grade Equivalent Score
Reading	110	99	90	96	9	1.8
Sounds/ Letters	40	40	100	99	9	4.2
Word Reading	40	34	85	84	7	1.4
Sentence Reading	30	25	83	95	8	1.7
Math	40	28	70	59	5	1.0
Environment	40	31	78	83	7	2.1
Listening	40	32	80	81	7	2.2
Basic Battery	190	159	84	89	8	1.7
Complete Battery	230	190	83	88	7	1.9

weakest point, he or she still outperformed 59 percent of the national norming group. Though a bit less precise, the stanines repeat that information. All of this would help a teacher design instruction that would further assist this able student.

Table 2 provides additional information by breaking down the categories into components and giving details not evident in the larger picture. The number omitted can be found, and comparisons can be made for each subcategory with the norming group as to whether the student was average, below average, or above average.

Table 2
Sample Elementary Score Breakdown

Content Name	Raw Score	Number of Questions	Number Answered	Below Average	Average	Above Average
Sounds and Letters	40	40	40			X
Auditory Perception	16	16	16			X
Word Reading	34	40	40			X

(continued)

Table 2 (continued)

Content Name	Raw Score	Number of Questions	Number Answered	Below Average	Average	Above Average
Sentence Reading	25	30	30			X
Kernel Sentences	13	13	13			X
Sentence Transformations	11	13	13			X
Two-Sentence Stories	1	4	4		X	

Information this detailed is in each child's permanent record to give subsequent teachers the information needed to plan effective, focused, individualized instruction.

TYPICAL PREPARATION PROGRAM FOR K–12 EXAMPLE: SAT/ACT WORKSHOP

Students in grades K–12 cannot pay attention in class as long as post–high school students; for them a two- to three-hour session is enough. This, of course, means that more sessions will be needed. About fifteen total hours will suffice for test preparation. (For elaboration and details on test preparation, see Chapter 4.)

Day One

The first day with the SAT/ACT students follows the format for the post–high school students except that it stops after the reading test. These younger students don't benefit from classes longer than about 2½ hours because their ability to concentrate is more limited. First I discuss the nature of the test, grading, and format, and then the discussion moves to general areas of health, test-taking techniques, item analysis, reading factors, and content knowledge concerns.

Normally I do not present the relaxation technique because it is seldom a serious concern with younger test takers. In fact, many K–12 students benefit from increased anxiety. For many test takers it is their low anxiety level that contributes to poor performance; they take standardized tests and do not really care how they do. Some schools have even planned activities that raise anxiety or engagement by offering successful classes a reward, such as a pizza party, for increased test performance.

I then administer the McGraw-Hill Basic Skills System reading test (see Chapter 4), which takes a little over an hour to complete.

At the end of the first class I also assign about twenty-five vocabulary words. For each word, I ask the students to learn a meaning and to be able to use it correctly in a sentence.

Day Two

At the beginning of this class I present the necessary math for the students to understand percentiles because that is the format of the reading test results. This enables each student to understand his or her own scores. When they understand their own strengths and weaknesses they can be engaged more easily in the remediation process.

Next, I present several of the student reading results on the board anonymously and discuss each, and then I pass out the score results. I immediately follow with the *Reading and Study Skills* book (Schmelzer and Christen, 1996 [1980]); see Chapter 4). Then the students get started with a few reading exercises aimed at increasing both reading speed and comprehension. The process is to read a selection, write down how many minutes and seconds it takes, answer four comprehension questions, translate the time into words per minute, and record both speed and comprehension on a chart. The process is repeated several times until each student is comfortable with the procedure.

Now is a good time to have the students write a twenty-five-minute sample essay in the SAT format, using the TO541 reminder presented earlier. I normally assign the same topic to each student and evaluate each effort using the feedback sheet found in the Appendix at the end of this book.

I am now ready to tackle some math. I try some basic concepts like the interrelationships among fractions, decimals, and percentages because questions often draw on these concepts. We work on some sample problems.

Finally, I administer a short test on the vocabulary words from the first class.

The following homework is assigned for the third class:

1. Do several more exercises from the reading book.

2. Learn twenty-five more vocabulary words.

3. Review the math done in class.

Day Three

I start this class with a couple of reading exercises from the book distributed at the second class. Students time themselves, answer the four questions, and record their results.

It is during this class that I help the students understand the structure of multiple-choice questions. I present the three types from Chapter 3 and we practice classification until the students can do it with considerable ease and accuracy.

Next, I return the essays written during the second class with annotations and a summary sheet (see the Appendix at the end of this book). Some will proceed to a second essay while others rewrite the first. Then I discuss some of the errors made on the initial essays. Usually it is handled by writing the sentence containing the error and asking for correction. A common error demonstrated this way might be subject-verb agreement. I show the student errors, discuss the correct forms, and give some more practice.

Math comes next. I pick another broad aspect, such as geometry, review the basics, and have the students work on some problems.

Finally, I hand back the first vocabulary test and administer a vocabulary test on the twenty-five words assigned in the second class.

The following homework is assigned for the fourth class:

1. Continue with some more exercises in the reading book.

2. Review the geometry covered.

3. Learn the next twenty-five words.

Day Four

Now the pattern is set. We start with a few more reading exercises from the *Reading and Study Skills* book. Each student records his or her results. I check for accuracy. Many of the students can now begin to see their own progress, which increases motivation. Then they take twenty-five minutes to write another essay.

For math it is a good time to present methods to read tables and graphs more efficiently. Many tests use graphic presentations because they tend to discriminate between students who understand from those who have simply memorized information.

Finally, I hand back the second vocabulary test and administer a vocabulary test on the twenty-five words assigned in the third class.

The following homework is assigned for the fifth class:

1. Do several more reading exercises.

2. Practice the graph and table exercises.

3. Learn twenty-five more vocabulary words.

Day Five

This class is low pressure and functions as a tapering-off session to give the students more confidence and to review the tools that the previous four classes have given them.

To continue the pattern already set, we begin with a few reading exercises. I then hand back the previous day's essays with feedback sheets, as well as the third vocabulary test.

Moving to the quantitative side, we discuss the important statistical concepts of mean, median, and mode. Students practice with some worksheets.

I then go over the plans they need to formulate for the last few days before taking the test. We talk about what is permitted in the test center and what is not. I have also found it helpful to have them visualize the test and formulate a time management plan to get through the various sections. Success or failure is often determined by the success a test taker has in managing time.

Finally, I administer a vocabulary test on the twenty-five words assigned in the fourth class.

CHECKLIST FOR THE EVALUATION OF A TEST PREPARATION PROGRAM

See Chapter 4 for the complete checklist.

REFERENCES

Anderson, L. W. 1995. Time, allocated, and instructional. In L. W. Anderson (Ed.), *International encyclopedia of teaching and teacher education* (2nd ed., pp. 204–207). Oxford: Pergamon Press.

Dewalt, M. W. 2006. *Amish education in the United States and Canada.* Lanham, MD: Rowman & Littlefield.

Friedman, M. I., Harwell, D. H., and Schnepel, K. C. 2006. *Effective instruction: A handbook of evidence-based strategies.* Columbia, SC: Institute for Evidence-Based Decision-Making in Education.

Friedman, M. I. et al. 2003. *Educators' handbook on effective testing.* Columbia, SC: Institute for Evidence-Based Decision-Making in Education.

Schmelzer, R. V., and Christen, M. L. 1996. *Reading and study skills.* [Revised edition.] Reading Rate Boosters, Book One. Dubuque, IA: Kendall/Hunt. (Originally published in 1980.)

6

Relevant Side Issues

INSTRUCTOR QUALIFICATIONS

Instruction plays a significant part in raising standardized test scores. While in an ideal world all teachers would be highly qualified, variation in instruction would still exist, partly influenced by the more subtle aspects of a teacher's own test performance. It is generally accepted that teachers who do well academically themselves tend to produce students who in turn also do well on tests. Darling-Hammond (1999) has summarized research on this topic in the following way: she used student achievement as the dependent variable and teacher characteristics as the independent variable. This data was drawn from three sources: various state policies, analyses of state policy making, and state achievement scores. She reported two primary findings: "First, while student demographic characteristics are strongly related to student outcomes at the state level, they are less influential in predicting achievement levels than variables assessing the quality of the teaching force. Second, when aggregated at the state level, teacher quality variables appear to be more strongly related to student achievement than class size, overall spending levels, teacher salaries (at least when unadjusted for cost of living differentials), or such factors as the statewide proportion of staff who are teachers" (Darling-Hammond, 1999, p. 38). She further clarified teacher quality by saying, "the percentage of teachers with full certification and a major in the field is a more powerful predictor of student achievement than teachers' education levels" and "other measures of certification status (e.g., the percent of teachers uncertified, the percent with full certification) are also strong correlates of student achievement" (ibid.). She concluded, "the effects of well-prepared teachers on student achievement can be stronger than the influences of student background factors, such as poverty, language background, and minority status" (ibid., p. 39).

Teacher licensure is an area of considerable concern because it has such a great impact on the actual supply of candidates for classroom positions. Most states have adopted a bilateral approach. First, courses are decided upon and required. That is, colleges and universities must offer them and require them for education degrees. Personnel transferring from out of state must meet these same requirements. Second, independent testing is often required. This testing usually has two tiers. Students must pass a preliminary, lower-level basic skills test for program admission (the PRAXIS I is normally used for this purpose). The second tier is composed of one or more PRAXIS II tests that focus on subject understanding in a particular field (e.g., elementary education, physical education, or special education). What states are really saying is that they do not trust institutions to produce highly qualified candidates without supervision. The usual effect of the testing is to reduce the number of education graduates as well as restrict the number of job applicants in the employment pool of any particular district. The effect of the testing requirements is most noticeable in the reduction in the number of minority candidates (Mitchell et al., 2001, p. 111).

Of greater concern to us here is the effect of this extensive testing on the quality of teachers. There is little doubt that the process weeds out those potential teachers who possess less knowledge and understanding of a content field. However, there is considerable doubt as to the extent that the tests restrict entrance into the field to effective teachers (Mitchell et al., 2001, p. 169). It is also likely that simply raising required test scores and/or increasing the number of required courses for certification will have no beneficial effect on student learning. The more likely effect would be to raise salaries. Some years ago the state of Mississippi raised the required PRAXIS test scores and expected to have more qualified teachers in classrooms and increased student performance as a result. When monitors went out to survey the teachers, they found that many more classes were being taught by permanent substitutes who were not certified at all. The changes had had an unanticipated negative effect: the attractiveness of raising required scores meant that there was virtually no cost to the state of Mississippi.

Highly effective teachers convey their attitudes and subtly different concepts, as well as a more challenging vocabulary, in instruction. Over time, all of these aspects of instruction are absorbed by students, producing better test scores.

These concerns can also be viewed from the standpoint of cognitive learning theory. One summary (Gordon et al., 2007, p. 100) lists three characteristics of high-quality instruction. The first involves setting up situations that enhance meaning. The second involves promotion of critical thinking. The third analyzes whether the instructor develops problem solving as a realistic class expectation. My students tell me that the above three characteristics are usually not reflected in their college classes. They are given material to learn, they learn it more or less successfully, and they repeat it on a test in order to pass.

One example of a serious teaching failure was told to me by a student in Virginia. She was having a terrible time with the PRAXIS test that included grammar and writing. Her real problem, she thought, was her junior high school English teacher, who made a deal with her class that she would not teach and would not give homework, but would give good grades if the students quietly managed themselves during her class. My student had her for two years and learned absolutely nothing. But just think: what eighth grader would refuse an offer like that?

TIME DEVOTED TO PREPARATION

The amount of time devoted to preparation is proportional to achievement. More productive time leads to greater improvement. A great deal of research has been done under the general label "Time on task." In discussing the task of maximizing teaching time, Friedman et al. (2006, p. 73) state: "The evidence indicates that the amount of time spent engaged in teaching activities enhances the academic achievement of students in elementary and secondary classrooms in the subject areas of English, reading, and mathematics. No evidence could be found to suggest that maximizing teaching time should not be stressed in all subject areas for all types of students including students in college, military, community, business, and adult education settings."

Other related strategies in the above book include:

Keeping Students on Task

Providing Ample Learning Time

Controlling Classroom Disruptions

In workshops I have led for ACT, SAT, and PRAXIS preparation, the length of time between the first and last class seems just as important as the number of actual contact hours. What has worked well for my students has been about fifteen hours of classroom time spread over about six to eight weeks, supplemented by about twelve hours per week of additional out-of-class study. Expressed another way, about 50 to 100 hours over two months yields good results.

TIME MANAGEMENT ON A TEST

It is perfectly possible to perform poorly on a given test simply through poor time management. Because most standardized tests are administered with strict time limits, constructive use of time can become a big issue.

To illustrate: No long ago I received an e-mail from a former student who had just taken the PRAXIS 0012, which is one of the essay tests in elementary education. Students have two hours in which to answer four evenly weighted essay (constructed response) questions. Logic would dictate spending about thirty minutes on each question. This is also the recommendation from the Educational Testing Service (ETS). My student had doubts about how well she had done because she spent one hour and forty-five minutes on the first two questions and only fifteen minutes on the last two! A better plan would have been to set fairly strict time limits on each of the four questions and maintain that plan. There is also another consideration: each constructed response is assigned only so many points. So, if you find the first question is one that you know well and can write on extensively, you will quickly meet the point of diminishing returns. That is, devoting extra time to create an exhaustive answer may not get you any more points. Once you hit the maximum, you simply can't get any more. Consequently, it is perfectly possible that this young lady maxed out her points on one of the first questions after thirty-five minutes. The additional time devoted to that question only resulted in lowering the points for one of the last two, which had the ultimate effect of lowering her total score.

Sometimes you need to be flexible with a plan to optimize a score. Several months ago I took the PRAXIS test for middle school social studies (0089). This is one of the new family of ETS tests that contains both multiple-choice and constructed response questions; the test is to be completed in two hours. ETS provides information on weighting, which strongly influences making a test plan. They say the ninety multiple-choice questions count for 75 percent of the grade, while the three essays count for 25 percent. This set up my initial plan of spending ninety minutes on the former and thirty on the latter. However (and that is an important word), I found that the multiple-choice questions went faster than anticipated; I had them completed after sixty minutes. This gave me a full twenty minutes for each of the essays instead of the ten I had planned, allowing me to create answers that were longer, broader, and deeper than originally planned. All three of these characteristics make for more points on a test of this kind, where the highest grades seem to be given to those answers that are in fact longer with greater detail. I would have had considerable trouble if I had elected to do the essay questions first because I would then have given each only ten minutes, and going back after the multiple-choice questions to elaborate would have been awkward and led to a lower score. From the plan I followed, I made a score of 198 out of a possible 200 points, much of which is attributable to having adopted a flexible time management plan.

Other tests that give students horrible time management problems are the four PRAXIS Principles of Learning and Teaching (PLT) tests. The main problem here is the format of the test. Students are given four long case studies with three essay questions for each (a total of twelve essays). In addition, there are twenty-four multiple-choice questions. All must be answered in two hours. ETS suggests that test takers spend twenty-five minutes on each case study and twenty minutes on the multiple-choice questions. This suggested time frame translates to a weighting of five-sixths for the case studies and one-sixth for the multiple-choice questions. Almost no test taker can gain more than a minute or two on the multiple-choice questions to devote to the essays. I have been told innumerable times how students would be caught at the end of the two hours with only two of the case studies complete. All those unfinished questions are calculated as zeros!

This time pressure creates its own response pattern. There is no time to consider an answer, outline thoughts, write a first draft, revise, and then produce a clean copy. The only thing to do is outline a few thoughts and then write one draft. The first draft has to be the final one. Many thoughtful, creative students find this frame-work onerous.

REINFORCEMENT FROM OTHER SUBJECTS

In Chapter 5 I discussed the limiting effect of narrowly focused classroom tests that allow students to learn a single approach and then repeat it to receive a satis-factory grade. Why not broaden school testing so that each test includes questions from previously learned material? This would help to create an ongoing review process.

It is not possible to extend skills across too many subjects. For example, if a school is concerned about writing ability, why not have the social studies essay answers graded by the English teacher also? Lately this has become an increased concern because, as mentioned previously, the current form of the SAT now in-cludes a section on writing. If students write correctly for all subjects, the learning will multiply. Likewise, if the construction of graphs is not confined to math class, but is extended to social studies and science, the lessons will be that much stronger. Another method is to use English class to write essays about science or social studies. Thus, students would get two grades, one for each subject. Reinforcement and coordination are the keys.

HELPFUL SOURCES

An excellent source of information about instructional strategies that have a positive effect on student learning is *Effective Instruction: A Handbook of Evidence-Based Strategies* (Friedman et al., 2006). This book includes student benefi-ciaries by grade and subject, learning achieved, recommended instructional techniques, cautions and comments, and generalizations, as well as an extensive reference list. Descriptions of the strategies appear below. It not an exaggeration to maintain that the success of *any* school is tied to the extent that it implements these straightforward, research-based strategies. In November 2007 this wonderfully useful book became available to individuals, schools, and districts through Larry Lezottte's Effective Schools Web site, www.effectiveschools.com. This format allows users to perform a search of all relevant research by subject and/or grade.

1. Taking Student Readiness into Account

Research completely supports the effectiveness of taking student readiness into account at any grade level and in any subject. Over 350 studies are cited that sup-port this strategy. An example of this might be found in math. Students who do not know the basics of math cannot be expected to advance to geometry or algebra with any success. I have often been asked to prepare students to pass the PRAXIS I math test, only to discover that they don't know the basics (for example, $8 \times 7 = 56$).

Others may simply not be able to do long division. Until those students step back and master those skills, no forward progress is possible. I could also imagine that a serious weakness in reading would mean that no serious study of literature could be undertaken.

2. Defining Instructional Expectations

Friedman et al. cite three steps necessary to the implementation of this objective. Teachers must define

The learning objective.

How to achieve the learning objective.

The performance criteria. (p. 36)

More than 350 studies support this strategy across grade levels and subjects. For elaboration, the classic article by Gagne (1962) summarizes how each of the above can be operationalized.

This strategy works in a logical manner to focus students on the task at hand and how to achieve it. They know where they are going, how to get there, and what the resulting grades will be.

3. Providing Instructional Evaluation

Effective evaluation enhances student achievement. Students will review and integrate previous instruction in order to perform well on a summative evaluation. Effective instruction will not only look back over instruction that has occurred, but will also allow a teacher to plan the next unit to maximize integration of the previous one.

The failure to utilize this strategy can be disastrous for many students. If they constantly fail to meet evaluation criteria and are not remediated, frustrations will rise that can only result in greater likelihood of dropping out (Friedman et al., 2006, p. 43). Over 290 studies are cited that support this strategy.

4. Providing Corrective Instruction

Providing students with immediate corrective instruction, activities, or tutoring can turn failure into success. Research shows how broadly this concept can be applied, across grades and across subjects. Students need to be assured that success is possible and that the means will be supplied. Together this encouragement, followed by immediate activities, provides the means to give most students a path to increased achievement. In some classrooms students can follow an erroneous procedure for quite some time before correction. They actually learn the error very well, to the detriment of future performance. This strategy emphasizes the application of immediate remediation before the "incorrect" learning occurs.

Imagine a student writing a five-paragraph essay on a subject to follow a particular format (e.g., in a 30-minute period). If the student writes a number of essays that do not meet the criteria, remediation is much more difficult than if it starts after the first.

Over 500 studies are cited in support of this strategy.

5. Keeping Students on Task

We have all done it: we have been in a class but our minds are miles away and we are not attending to anything that is happening in the room. In short, we have derailed the learning process. The less this happens, the better are the results.

A somewhat comical but apt story related to these distractions found its way into a news column a short while ago. A business professor at Roanoke College (Virginia) halted his lecture on market research when he heard a cell phone ring. This was after he had announced a zero tolerance policy for the devices. The professor asked the student for the phone, pulled a hammer out of his briefcase, and proceeded to destroy the offending instrument (The New Class Struggle: Hang Up and Learn, 2007).

The same story reported that wireless service in college classrooms is now up to 60 percent! Concomitantly, cell phone, e-mail, instant messaging, and social networking are accessed by a majority of students *during* class. This usage has even prompted the development of the SynchronEyes program, which allows a professor to monitor all computer usage in a classroom and freeze all machines with one click of a mouse (ibid.).

Research (ninety-five studies) supports the following activities to combat inattention:

1. Correlate all assignments to the objective.

2. Provide work for which the students have the prerequisite skills.

3. See that the instruction is logical and well planned, not haphazard.

4. Show students how to do the work—demonstrate the skills. If you want students to produce an informative panel discussion, show a video of one done correctly.

5. Make sure each student is ready to perform an independent activity before starting.

6. Correlate the subsequent activity to the prior demonstration. The greater the correlation, the greater the possibility for success.

7. Plan for the activity to follow the demonstration closely. The greater the

time lapse, the greater the possibility that students will lose the connection. Make them contiguous.

8. Make sure that directions are detailed. In chapters 4 and 5 of this volume, I show how I ask students to write an essay using the mental prompt of TO541. This gives them a reminder of all the expected steps in writing a good essay.

9. Before engaging in an assigned activity, elicit from students clarification of the desired work. A question-and-answer format works well. For item 8 above, I would ask again: What does each part entail? How many parts to the outline? How many paragraphs? How many sentences in each paragraph?

10. Supervise the students as they work. Circulate, comment, entertain questions, and provide correction. Some years ago a movie appeared containing a sequence that showed the extreme opposite of this step. A teacher had his desk in the rear of the room. As each class filed in, students picked up seatwork from his desk, completed this work at their seats, and placed the completed assignments in a class basket as they left. The teacher died one day while reading a newspaper at his desk. Classes proceeded with no alteration of procedure because his "absence" was not even noticed.

11. Keep disruptions minimized; they can ruin instruction in any class period. These can take the form of student interactions, intercom announcements, or even normal transitions like passing out materials or taking up assignments. (Friedman et al., 2006, p. 68)

6. Maximizing Teaching Time

Increased instructional time correlates positively with increased learning. However it is done, this increase will have positive results. Sixty-eight studies are cited in support of this strategy. These involve the following six tactics:

1. Make each classroom a learning-centered environment where the teacher is directed toward presenting material, giving demonstrations of related performance, and monitoring student activities.

2. Minimize the assignment of independent learning activities, where distractions are greatest.

3. Avoid assigning "busy work."

4. Do the planning and organizing of instruction outside the class period.

5. Avoid nonacademic activities during class time—no sports talk, no music, no socializing.

6. Minimize outside administrative distractions, such as announcements, and

confine those to specific times during the day, such as homeroom period. (Friedman et al., 2006, pp. 74–75)

7. Providing Ample Learning Time

Over 450 research studies support this activity across a broad range of subjects and grades.

Time to present material, time to allow students to process it, time to practice it, and even time to make errors are all necessary. Three tactics are interrelated:

1. Time to allow students to utilize information through assignments should be allocated.
2. Remediation time should also be planned for those who are unable to do the previous step.
3. Total time to absorb a lesson needs to be planned to encompass the whole range of assigned activities. (Friedman et al., 2006, p. 80)

All of us have encountered classes that have done poorly with these three recommendations. I recall teaching statistics classes in summer school, where time was a terrible problem. When there was a class every day, students simply did not have time to process and think about the previous day's concept, which may have been poorly grasped, before the next class arrived and they were required to build on that concept. Having class once a week worked much better because in the intervening six days students could wrap their minds around a concept with greater success.

In spring 2007 I worked with a math teacher who told me about another math teacher at his school who had resigned early in the school year because of great classroom problems. This teacher had covered a great amount of material in the first week of school. The director of the math department even commented that what she had covered in less than a week took him over a month to teach. I think the former math teacher had simply run through material at a great rate and overwhelmed the students to the point of rebellion. They could not imagine going through a whole year in the same manner. The result was failure for the teacher, for the students, and for the school, all because of an unwillingness or an inability to implement this strategy.

Another problem that arises in the implementation of this strategy is the perceived obligation teachers often feel to "cover" material. How often have you heard history students explain why they, for example, don't know much about twentieth-century history? They recall how that class covered all the last chapters in the book the last week of the semester. The teacher had gone through earlier periods in a relaxed and thorough manner and then had simply run out of time. This caused the compressing of those last chapters into too short a time period.

8. Providing Transfer of Learning Instruction

Each day we are required to apply previous information to a new context. Some subjects, like math, are more rigorous in this regard than others. Students cannot learn to work fractions if they do not know the basics of addition, subtraction, multiplication, and division.

The following eight tactics are referenced by the research:

1. Make sure that students possess the requisite skills.

2. Have students assess themselves to see if they possess the necessary skills.

3. Teach relevant procedures for success.

4. As they learn an activity, have students look forward to ways they may be able to utilize that learning in other situations.

5. Help students correlate tasks and procedures.

6. Show students how a procedure might be utilized in a different but related task.

7. Teach students to think about previous procedures and to select one that might work in a new situation.

8. Give students practice in selecting a procedure to utilize. (Friedman et al., 2006, pp. 91–92)

Math teachers follow this procedure often when they ask, "Who can think of another way to solve this problem?"

Over 240 studies support this strategy across both grades and subjects.

9. Providing Decision-Making Instruction

When students are given instruction in how to choose and implement decision-making activities, their academic performance is enhanced.

Seven steps can be broken out for this strategy:

1. Make sure that assignments are clear and constraints are noted.

2. Break down assignments to clarify the component pieces.

3. Review approaches that students have employed previously.

4. Evaluate previous approaches for an assessment of possible relevance and success.

5. Make a proposed selection based on item 4 above.

6. Check to see if the chosen procedure contains any foreseeable defects.

7. Finalize the selection. (Friedman et al., 2006, p. 107)

I think of some of the simplified ways teachers use this procedure. After I assign some vocabulary for a class, I usually ask students how they have approached a task like this before. I even make some suggestions that they may not have considered, like putting the words and definitions on tape and listening to them again and again as they drive. Some find this last approach especially attractive because it does not involve finding any additional study time but simply puts previously dead time to work.

This strategy is supported by 202 studies.

10. Providing Prediction and Problem-Solving Instruction

Seventy-two studies support prediction and problem-solving instruction to increase student performance at all grade levels. These break down the process into four stages:

Stage 1: diagnosing problems. A good diagnosis leads logically to some steps toward that goal. For example, if the goal is to improve a score on the LSAT by ten points, the subject knows that out of the 100 questions, about ten more need to be answered correctly. Analysis of the question types will also narrow the focus to particular types, such as analysis or main idea questions. Further analysis may also show that broadening vocabulary will give more correct answers.

Stage 2: predicting solutions. Here the person posits certain activities to move toward the goal. These may be based on previous related activities and degree of success or on the recommendations of persons who have had extensive experience with similar problems. In this case, the subject may look back to high school, when he or she may have taken certain steps to increase an SAT score. The subject may also consider the LSAT like a course giving trouble. How did the subject respond to that challenge? What kind of time was invested? Was tutoring needed?

Stage 3: implementing solutions. Here the subject undertakes certain steps from stage 2 above and puts them into action.

Stage 4: assessing achievement. Here the outcome is evaluated. Was the goal reached? If not, was there progress in the desired direction? How about the cost-benefit analysis? Was the increase worth the cost? Could the goal have been achieved at a lower cost or effort? If the goal has not been met, the subject can recycle the process and work through the steps again. (Friedman et al., 2006, pp. 121–123)

11. Providing Contiguity

Over 490 studies support this particular strategy across all grades and subjects. It was even found effective with special needs students.

Timing seems to be the critical factor in this strategy. That is, if a teacher wished students to see the relationship between two concepts, they should be presented in proximity. Here is also where homework, creatively designed, can provide immediate practice on concepts taught that day. It also supports that old educational practice of many veteran teachers who attempted to correct papers and return them promptly the next day. This contiguity of product and evaluation works well. When is the best time to go over the words just given on a vocabulary test? Right after the last paper is handed in, because it is at exactly that point when the student is most receptive of correction—the "Teachable Moment."

12. Utilizing Repetition Effectively

This strategy is supported by 183 studies across a wide range of grades and subjects. It includes the following five instructional tactics, which broadly perform two functions. First, a preview of a lesson will alert students about what is to follow and make the succeeding lesson have the character of an enhanced repetition. Second, actually repeating previous material provides a strong reinforcement of that learning. Most teachers do a great deal of the latter at the beginning of a school year. They repeat, in synopsis form, previously learned material. I can hear an Algebra II student stating that the first few weeks of school were no challenge because they were simply a review of Algebra I.

First instructional tactic. The teacher repeats what is to be covered in the next lesson. First she might say, "Next week we will start on the events leading to the Civil War." Then, "Now we are almost ready to start on the causes of the Civil War." And finally, "Now we are ready to learn about how the Civil War started." All of these serve as a repetition of a theme and get the class focused on what is to follow.

Second instructional tactic. Here, actual repetition of the task by the students takes place. Teachers may have classroom assignments that are similar or give homework that reinforces a particular lesson previously taught.

Third instructional tactic. Here, the frequency of repetitions is increased. This always seems to enhance learning and make it more resistant to forgetting.

Fourth instructional tactic. The most effective repetition is varied in nature. Frequent post-testing will enhance learning.

Fifth instructional tactic. A preliminary test will enhance subsequent learning. It serves to strengthen learning and to make it more resistant to forgetting.

Repetition also would seem to enhance teacher performance itself. The second time a lesson is given, it will be improved and will work more smoothly. Think of the difference between first-year and second-year teachers. In that first year, everything is new. All the lessons, concepts, and ideas are being presented and explained by that person for the first time. However, the more experienced teacher is able to make minor adjustments and modifications that greatly enhance student learning. He or she is constantly thinking, "That didn't work very well last time. What can I do to improve?" Or, "That worked well last time, but if I added this it would be greatly improved." Repetition even clarifies the concepts in a teacher's mind (Friedman et al., 2006, pp. 139–140).

13. Utilizing Unifiers

Over 370 articles support this strategy across all grades and a wide range of subjects. Two general approaches were used: (1) unifiers supplied by the instructor and (2) unifiers developed by the student. Whichever way they are developed, they give students a unified way to perceive material that is more resistant to forgetting than trying to remember material that is conceived of as being merely a collection of discrete facts (Friedman et al., 2006, p. 153).

Sometimes teachers could use unifiers like this: in mathematics, the various transformations of fractions, decimals, and percents can be taught as a whole series of discrete rules—or better, taught as a unified, interrelated whole. Using the latter approach, a teacher can be assured that students will be more successful and have longer retention with greater accuracy than if the concepts are all taught as separate, discrete rules.

There are instances where the teacher presents material in such a disjointed, confusing manner that students must develop their own organizers. I can recall a graduate statistics course that functioned in exactly that manner. The confusing manner of presentation without any use of overriding principles forced me to supply them in the form of a study outline that was finally copyrighted and published. I had to provide the unification when the instructor did not.

In an analogous way, Albert Einstein worked his whole life to develop a comprehensive theory that would explain gravity, magnetism, and the forces within the atom. He sought this because he was convinced that God would not have created a world that was not ruled by deep underlying mathematical principles that were elegantly simple. This same pursuit was also his motivation in discovering both of his theories of relativity (special and general). Initially, he even considered using the term "invariability" instead of "relativity" to reflect this viewpoint.

14. Providing One-to-One Tutoring

Over 500 studies support the validity of this approach for all instructional levels and subjects.

This is potentially the most effective method available for either instruction or remediation. Tutoring is able to raise the performance of students two standard deviations over those with more conventional instruction. That would put their tests at the ninety-eighth percentile! They have another advantage in that less remediative instruction is needed (Friedman et al., 2006, p. 175).

Though the tutoring may be performed by a regular instructor, effective instruction may also be provided by qualified teaching assistants or even fellow students. A form of individualized tutoring is at the heart of the current success of home-schooling.

15. Utilizing Reminders

One hundred seventy-three studies support the efficacy of this strategy across grade levels and subjects.

Have you ever wondered how many days there are in the current month? My first recourse is to say the old rhyme in my head that goes: "Thirty days hath September, April, June, and November, etc." to get the answer. I am utilizing a reminder to aid recall. Another one that I use is the sentence "Kids can always act so easily" to recall the six levels of Bloom's Taxonomy in the correct order (Knowledge, Comprehension, Application, Analysis, Synthesis, and Evaluation). A student of mine used a mnemonic device to remember Bloom but said "Kissing comes after a special evening." She seemed to find hers easier to recall than mine. Another one commonly used by math students is "Please excuse my dear Aunt Sally." This cute reminder gives a student the order of operations from left to right. The words stand for the following: parentheses, exponents, multiplication, division, addition, and subtraction.

Teachers can encourage students to develop their own reminders to recall essential information. The process of developing the applications will be helpful for the immediate task and give students another tool to use as their lives as learners advance. Medical students have whole reams of mnemonic devices to recall nerves, blood vessels, and other parts of the body.

16. Utilizing Teamwork

Eight steps may be incorporated in the development of successful teamwork.

Step 1 assess each student's readiness for an activity of this type.

Step 2 assigns individuals to teams of four or five.

Step 3 sets aside time for team-building activities where individuals become better acquainted with each other.

Step 4 uses the dual approach of addressing the total group as well as individuals regarding their responsibilities.

Step 5 is when the group starts to function and begins to plan approaches to the solution of the assignment.

Step 6 is the development of the plan with the assistance of the teacher.

Step 7 is the evaluation, both as a group and for individuals, of the project.

Step 8 is the wrap-up and recognition of tasks well performed. (Friedman et al., 2006, p. 201)

When looking at this strategy it is important to note that life is more like a group project than an individual test, so student benefits from this may extend far into their futures. Imagine the student who finishes college and goes to work for a large computer company that installs hardware and software for management of large warehouses. Each installation requires the joint work of many persons who must be able to coordinate for the success of the project. There is a constantly shifting set of problems requiring constantly changing group members to solve them; communication becomes extremely important. A real-life situation like this requires graduates who are able to function as members of a team; therefore, actually teaching teamwork skills and giving students practice in carrying them out is essential.

Over 380 studies support this strategy across a broad spectrum of subjects.

17. Reducing Student/Teacher Ratio Below 21 to 1

One hundred ninety-three studies support this finding across grade levels and across subjects.

One may also think of strategy 14 (One-to-One Tutoring) and homeschooling as class size reduction. However, the benefits begin to be measurable as class sizes drop below 21. This means that although schools, districts, and colleges may view reducing class size as a worthy goal, benefits may not be realized immediately. For example, if a district has twenty-seven students in an average fourth grade class and decides to gradually reduce this by five, the expenses will mount with the hiring of additional teachers and potentially with the addition of new classrooms, but an increase in student performance will not be seen until the mean drops below 21. Results of class size reduction will not be immediate and may not occur at all.

I can recall teaching ninth grade social studies classes in Maryland that had forty-five students. Each of those could have been split in half with the concomitant doubling of expenses without any predictable increase in student achievement.

18. Clarifying Communication

Everyone has had experience with poor communication. Think of that painful television interview with the star athlete. The mumbling, the repeated "you know," and the clichés all interfere with the presentation of clear thoughts. Then there is the classic political speech that is entertaining but devoid of content. Both are examples of unclear communication.

Over 125 studies support this strategy across grades and subjects. The following are helpful suggestions derived from the research in this field.

1. Provide clear examples. Poor writing and speaking often stays in the abstract without giving the concrete examples that help someone follow the train of thought. Many ministers regularly use examples and anecdotes for illustration.

2. When speaking, avoid those annoying space fillers that distract an audience, such as "You know."

3. Keep to the subject. Insertion of the irrelevant will distract an audience.

4. Avoid vagueness. Give exact criteria, precise steps, and concrete information.

5. Keep your audience informed of the relationships you are presenting with transitional phrases like "The last item is" and "There were four cases of: . . . 1, 2, 3, 4." Then continue to lay out sequences or procedures in an orderly way. Lead the audience along with sequencing words. Again, using sermons as an example, most ministers will tell you the theme, discuss it, and at the end summarize it. You can tell the end is near when you hear the words "In conclusion" or "Finally."

6. Remember to include relevance and clear presentations of cause and effect. If you are discussing types of multiple-choice questions, use examples drawn from the actual test that will be administered.

7. Vary the approaches to clarify a concept. Wherever possible, give examples of reports, term papers, and projects. Define expectations. Now more than ever, a classroom teacher has resources only dreamed of a decade ago. Think of the computer and Internet sources now available.

8. Ask if you are understood. Keep up a constant flow of questions that find out whether your audience has been "left behind." The Socratic Method is as ancient as Athens but as relevant as today. Good teachers become adept at reading a class. They know when the thread has been lost and modify the presentation accordingly. They back up, clarify, add examples, and have students summarize.

9. Avoid using a complex or highly technical vocabulary that is above the audience.

10. Show the relevance of content to student lives. For example, although the American Civil War was over 140 years ago we are still seeing consequences.

11. Vary the presentation mode utilizing different senses. (Friedman et al., 2006, p. 224)

19. Utilizing Question and Answer Instruction

Two hundred forty-six studies support this strategy across most subject areas. These studies suggest the following implementation:

1. Preplan many of the questions.
2. Make the asking of questions integral to the presentation.
3. Entertain answers as questions are asked. That is, no rhetorical questions.
4. Note incorrect answers and remediate to give better understanding.
5. Note correct answers and give praise. (Friedman et al., 2006, p. 235)

20. Utilizing Computerized Instruction

This strategy is supported by 202 studies across a wide range of grades and subjects.

Implementation of computerized instruction is a great deal more than turning students loose with a computer. The integration of this resource needs to be made with the lessons to be learned. The following seven steps outline that procedure:

1. Decide on an appropriate program.
2. Acquaint the students with its operation and options.
3. Decide on an appropriate individual entry point.
4. Have students proceed with the program.
5. Check that each student is making desired progress.
6. Have students move forward to succeeding steps.
7. Recycle through steps 4–6 until desired learning has taken place. (Friedman et al., 2006, p. 240)

One of the advantages of a computer is that students must give constant responses. They are prompted to respond to questions or use the mouse to move to the next page. In a sense, computerized instruction is similar to tutoring. In both, constant responses must be made. The second advantage of a computer is that it is tireless. It will repeat a question or give a correction again and again. It does not lose patience or good humor, as a live teacher might.

21. Utilizing Demonstrations

Five hundred seventy-eight research articles support this strategy across most subject areas.

Each of us has had experience with this mode of instruction. Almost without exception we have found it helpful. Many years ago I asked one of my students how to tune up a lawn mower. He just said, "Bring the mower and the points to school and I will show you." He did that over thirty years ago and I could still do it easily today. The lessons taught can cross several sensory modalities to make the instruction very persistent. In my example, the visual, the auditory, and the tactile all combined for an excellent learning experience.

Vocational schools excel in this type of instruction. Quite a number of building trades programs actually build houses. It is one thing to read a textbook and make a few building components, but quite another to build a house correctly that will ultimately be sold for people to enjoy. When something is not right in the latter case, it must be ripped out and corrected.

QUESTIONABLE STRATEGIES

In addition to the helpful strategies listed above, the following were found *not* to be helpful:

1. Matching student–teacher field-dependent/field-independent cognitive styles.
2. Ability grouping students.
3. Providing whole language instruction.
4. Providing reinforcements.
5. Portfolio testing. (Friedman et al., 2006, pp. 265–282)

Many schools will find that student performance can be raised as much by discontinuing some practices, such as the five above, as by adopting others.

INSTRUCTIONAL AIDS

The following six instructional aids might also be considered:

1. Controlling Classroom Disruptions

Over 150 studies support the efficacy of reducing disruptions. Fifty of the above studies recommend the following steps, which you see implemented in many classrooms:

1. Post rules of conduct on the first day of class.
2. Use a few (perhaps five) simple rules.
3. Check students' knowledge of the rules.
4. Use rules and provide consequences with little disruption of instruction.

5. Communicate violations both verbally and nonverbally. (Friedman et al., 2006, p. 286)

2. Developing Teaching Proficiency

To become more proficient, teachers should learn the twenty-one strategies described above, either as part of teacher preservice training or as in-service programs after employment. These strategies can be learned and will impact on student achievement (see Friedman et al., 2006, chapter 25).

3. Preschool Instruction

The short-term and long-term positive effects of preschool are striking. Competent preschool teachers are able to provide these young children with the kind of academic foundation that gives them a clear advantage over students who do not have this background. Many, if not all, of the previous strategies can be successfully incorporated in preschool instruction (see Friedman et al., 2006, chapter 26).

4. Developing Preventive Tutoring Programs

Many students could be prevented from failing if preventive tutoring were employed. This is actually a special application of strategy 14 above.

For most teachers this means the enlistment of another person to perform the specialized instruction who is first informed of the precise weaknesses and then given the resources and time to do the tutoring (see Friedman et al., 2006, chapter 27).

5. Remedial Tutoring Programs

Remedial tutoring is for learning problems that are clinical in nature and involves specific, regimented programs for students who have diagnosed learning disabilities.

Included are such options as the Orton-Gillingham Instructional Program, the Wilson Reading System, TEACH, Programmed Tutorial Reading, the Wallach Tutoring Program, Reading Recovery, Success for All Language Tutoring, the Lindamood-Bell Clinical Instruction Program, and the Laubach Literacy Program (Friedman et al., 2006, pp. 314–324).

The Laubach Literacy Program is the basis for most adult literacy programs. Teachers or volunteers working in these programs are required to learn and use this technique for teaching that particular group.

6. Instructional Testing and Evaluation

The course of instruction should include the detailed gathering of information about student skills so that the student may pass along to another level or may be recycled to relearn specific precisely defined skills. This may include the administration of standardized criterion-related tests or skillfully prepared teacher tests. Whichever yields the best information should be used. I have had a number of students who would have benefited greatly from the application of this concept. I recall students who never really learned the multiplication tables and in all the subsequent years worked around the problem without solving it.

Thus, there are many ways that instructional practices may be improved. Most do not require the expenditure of any significant funds; some may require additional supplies at a modest cost. However, some practices, such as ability grouping, have been hallowed by long practice in spite of being ineffective. Here, change would require a considerable community education effort to garner support for it.

REFERENCES

Darling-Hammond, L. 1999. Teacher quality and student achievement: A review of state policy evidence. Document R-99-1. Seattle, WA: Center for the Study of Teaching and Policy.

Friedman, M. I., Harwell, D. H., and Schnepel, K. C. 2006. *Effective instruction: A handbook of evidence-based strategies.* Columbia, SC: Institute for Evidence-Based Decision-Making in Education.

Friedman, M. I. et al. 2003. *Educators' handbook on effective testing.* Columbia, SC: Institute for Evidence-Based Decision-Making in Education.

Gagne, R. M. 1962. The acquisition of knowledge. *Psychological Review,* 69(4), 355–365.

Gordon, E. E., Morgan, R. R., O'Malley, C. J., and Ponticell, J. 2007. *The tutoring revolution: Applying research for best practices, policy implications, and student achievement.* Lanham, MD: Rowman & Littlefield.

Mitchell, K. J. et al. 2001. *Testing teacher candidates: The role of licensure tests in improving teacher quality.* Washington, DC: National Academy Press.

The new class struggle: Hang up and learn. 2007. *State Newspaper* (Columbia, SC), November 9, p. A11.

7

The Role of Tutoring

Tutoring is undoubtedly the best method for instruction and test preparation. Imagine two SAT preparation sessions—one with fifty students and another with just one. In the large assembly, many students will be distracted with wandering minds much of the time, whereas the single student will be on task almost every minute. In the large group setting, most questions that come up in students' minds will go unasked and, of course, unanswered.

Even though tutoring is a powerful tool to enhance instruction, an energetic, able classroom teacher can achieve nearly the same results when teaching a full class group. She is able to monitor each student and to sense exactly when any one student is confused or distracted. The result is that nearly all of the students are on track and learning most of the time. Understandably, only a small proportion of teachers can function at this high level, but these few can serve as positive examples for other educators because of their ability to transform an ordinary classroom into an inspiring place where instruction is nearly individualized. Functioning in this manner is utterly demanding and leaves a teacher completely exhausted at the end of a long day. I recall a math teacher who functioned in this manner, teaching Advanced Placement high school math. He often told me that at the end of the day he would leave school, go out to his car, sit down, and not have the energy to turn the key to drive the short distance home. That is exactly the level of energy expended and the degree of focus that an individualized approach demands of an instructor.

Tutoring is not a simple or undemanding process. A long session will leave both participants drained because of the constant attention the process demands. I have found that practical limits are reached after four or five hours in a day and that additional time does not yield much additional value.

Changing pace, moving around, and modifying the approach will all allow a tutor to maximize efficiency.

A skillful tutor can track the student's thinking minute by minute and refocus as necessary. I can remember instructing a student on the key words in a multiple-choice question and explaining what they meant. We were working on the word "except." She said correctly that it meant to choose the incorrect option. However, she proceeded to look at the alternatives and indicated the one she felt was "correct." It was, but she had forgotten that she was looking for the "incorrect" answer. I can imagine that she did the same thing on the test, missing many questions unnecessarily. If I had been teaching her in a larger group setting, I would not have been able to focus on that specific error to show her how to refocus her thinking or even to correct her. In another case I had a student who needed the PRAXIS I math review. As I worked with her, I quickly found that she did not know basic math (e.g., $7 + 5 = 12$ or $8 \times 7 = 56$). As we worked on problems I could see her fingers twitching—she was counting for an answer. I went over some procedures but had to tell her that until the root problem was solved, no real progress could be made. In a classroom setting I never could have discovered the real problem.

Historically, much of instruction has been in the form of tutoring. Families would hire a tutor who would probably live with them and who would be responsible for the education of the children. This is a tradition that goes back to the days of ancient Greece. Alexander the Great had Aristotle as his tutor in the fourth century B.C.! A modern adaptation of this tradition is in the growing trend toward homeschooling. Some observers have been amazed that homeschooled students are now beginning to win national competitions in spelling and geography. However, it is no surprise to those who understand both the effectiveness and efficiency of tutoring.

One complexity in the theoretical analysis of tutoring is that there seem to be two main effects in play. The first is that of class size. There is clear evidence that student performance is enhanced as class size is lowered below twenty-one (see Chapter 17, "Reducing Student/Teacher Ratio Below 21 to 1," in Friedman et al., 2006). The ultimate reduction is to a class size of one, which is one-on-one tutoring.

The second effect is that tutoring seems to be instruction of a somewhat different kind. That is, the benefit of reducing the number of students down to one is enhanced because the nature of the tutor-to-tutee relationship is different from that of teacher to student. Gordon et al. (2007) refer to this as the "less is more" effect. This seems to contradict the Carroll (1963) model of instruction, where greater amounts of instruction are associated with higher achievement. For example, when instructional time in a class is increased, achievement is increased. Tutoring seems more efficient because fewer hours are required to produce superior results. Gordon et al. discuss the following factors that help to explain the success of tutoring:

1. Increased time on task.

2. Provision of quality instruction.

3. Alignment of tutoring curriculum with regular classroom curriculum.

4. Greater social (personal) involvement between tutor and tutee.

5. Provision of immediate and relevant feedback.

6. Positive alignment between what the student knows and the instructional tasks. (Gordon et al., 2007, p. 162)

Especially interesting are the first, fourth, and fifth factors. A student being tutored is constantly on task. Minds simply have no chance to wander. The fourth factor recognizes the intensely personal nature of the one-on-one contact, where personalities have a chance to interact in ways that almost never exist in a group setting. And the fifth factor recognizes that errors are caught almost immediately and correct responses can be constantly recognized with praise, which is difficult to do in a classroom.

Tutoring may also be viewed from three theoretical perspectives:

1. Tutoring as the primary mode of instruction.

2. Tutoring to prevent failure.

3. Remedial tutoring using stand-alone programs to address fundamental weaknesses in specifically defined populations.

Without any doubt, tutoring has a solid theoretical base, but is it practical for test preparation in the real world, with real people preparing for real tests? The following note from a student came to me after she had completed one day of concentrated tutorial work. Her joy and exuberance spills out with her every word.

Thank you.

I'm still on my pink cloud and want to stay there a while!

Dr. Hatch,

Thank you for all of your help. Your tutoring, direction, guidance, insight, and experience really enabled me to pass both PRAXIS II tests the FIRST TIME (sorry, maybe that is obnoxious, but I'm very excited and proud of myself—I worked very hard), and I couldn't have done it without you.

Although I had only 15 minutes left for the last two essay questions, I remembered at the beginning of the 0012 test that YOU SAID to write and write and write all that I knew on the essays. That is what I did regarding those first two questions, the content of which I knew the best. That made a big difference. If I had not known that, I would have assumed the Powers that Be would have preferred my writing to be short and concise.

Thank you so much!

I hope I am on this cloud for a week or two. It's been a long while since I've been on one! (Personal communication, reprinted with permission.)

TUTORING AS A PRIMARY MODE OF INSTRUCTION

This is the classical form of instruction, where one tutor teaches one or more students as the only or primary source of lessons. One of the oldest known examples is also one of the most successful. Alexander the Great grew up in the fourth century B.C. His father, Philip II, was one of the foremost statesmen and generals of his age and had led his small mountainous country of Macedon in northern Greece to prominence. Philip was able to persuade Aristotle come to Macedon to tutor his son (Alexander the Great, 2007). Before deciding to accept this position, Aristotle had spent many years in Plato's Academy and with Theophrastus in Asia Minor, studying botany and zoology. In fact, some maintain that Aristotle was the last man to have studied all known subjects of his age (Aristotle, 2007). What a person to have as a tutor! What credentials! Among the broad range of subjects he wrote on were aesthetics, ethics, government, metaphysics, politics, psychology, rhetoric, and theology.

A more modern form of this kind of tutoring is the current homeschooling movement so prevalent in English-speaking countries since the 1970s. The roots of the movement go back to the beginnings of compulsory education. Massachusetts began the trend in 1789, and by 1900 it was the general policy. Modern opposition to homeschooling was ignited by John Holt's book, *How Children Fail* (1964). Ray and Dorothy Moore (1975) provided the academic underpinning of the nascent movement. The Department of Education estimates that 1.1 million students were taught at home in 2003 (Institute of Education Sciences, 2004). Another source put the figure as high as 2.4 million by 2006, or about 4 percent of students (National Home Education Research Institute, 2007).

Of more concern to us in this discussion is the academic performance of those millions of homeschooled students. One research group puts those students 30 to 37 percentile points above other students across all subjects (National Home Education Research Institute, 2007). Stated differently, they would be approximately one standard deviation above their more conventionally taught students. Interestingly, the level of difference holds across all minorities and genders. Performance gaps that have troubled public schools so much seem to disappear (ibid.).

TUTORING TO PREVENT FAILURE

This type of tutoring is aimed at forestalling failure and does not take the place of conventional instruction. The role that tutoring may serve was highlighted by the personal experience of Karin Klein (2006), an editorial writer for the *Los Angeles Times*. In 1968, while attending Walt Whitman Junior High in Yonkers, New York, Klein tutored a fellow student, Johnny Patrillo, in algebra. Klein recently reflected on this peer-tutoring experience:

I thought about Johnny again as I read The Times' series this week on L.A.'s dropout problem. Algebra, the reporter found, is an insurmountable stumbling block for many high school students.

What struck me was that the reasons why Johnny can't do algebra in L.A. today are remarkably similar to why Johnny Patrillo couldn't do algebra almost four decades ago in Yonkers, N.Y. . . .

Things looked pretty hopeless to both of us those first couple of sessions. . . . Then, as we took it down to each step of each little calculation, the trouble became clear. Johnny somehow had reached ninth grade without learning the multiplication tables. . . .

As Johnny tried to work algebraic equations, his arithmetic kept bringing up weird results. But at least we knew where to start. We spent about half of those early sessions on multiplication drills. . . . Today's failing high school students . . . bring the same scanty skills to algebra class, according to The Times' series. . . .

Who can focus on the step-by-step logic of peeling back an equation until "x" is bared when it involves arithmetic that comes slow and slippery, always giving a different answer to the same calculation?

Yet in all these decades, the same school structure that failed Johnny goes on, dragging kids through the grades even though they don't master the material from the year before. . . .

What I learned from Johnny . . . children's skills are all over the map, yet we corral them into second grade, third grade and so forth, where everyone moves at one pace in all subjects. . . . If they're not getting it, give them extra tutoring, but don't push them forward until they're ready. . . . It requires a sea change in thinking. (Klein, 2006, p. B15, in Gordon et al., 2007, pp. 212–213)

Before Klein used Johnny's name in her story, she called him to get permission. She learned that he had died a year and a half earlier, leaving behind his wife, Joann, and four children. The eldest is a doctor, the second a teacher. The teenage daughter wants to become a journalist.

Johnny became an auto mechanic. "He loved math, and you know auto repair involves a lot of math," Joann told her. One last thing his wife related about Johnny: He was "incredibly fast at multiplication" (Gordon et al., 2007, p. 212).

The long anecdotal reference above clearly illustrates a number of positive characteristics about tutoring:

1. It does not necessarily need to be performed by an expert adult.

2. The level of success can be exceptionally high.

3. The mastery can be long lasting.

4. The process may be life changing for *both* participants.

There are some forms of tutoring that function in the gray area between these first two types. That is, they function in some ways as stand-alone instruction and in some ways to remediate shortcomings of traditional instruction. I think test preparation tutorials function this way. Some persons need comprehensive assistance across the whole breadth of a test; this case falls more into the first category of tutoring. Others need only a bit of prescriptive instruction in a few areas to gain mastery. Many of my preparation students fall here. I can recall one student taking the Chemistry, Physics and General Science PRAXIS who asked me at the first session whether he could write in the test booklet. When I said he could, he responded that now he knew how to pass. In the PRAXIS administration directions the proctor says, "do not write the answers in the test booklet but on the answer sheet." This requirement, I believe, absolves the Educational Testing Service from any responsibility to transfer answers written in the test booklet to the answer sheet.

Another form of tutoring has become a successful business model for companies like Sylvan Learning. They provide assistance of two main types:

1. Tutoring to improve classroom performance on subjects such as reading or math. Grade gain guarantees are even made.
2. Test preparation assistance for tests such as the SAT or ACT.

The regular Sylvan instructional format is for the tutor to sit "inside" a short curved table with one to six tutees arranged around the "outside." This physical arrangement fosters a constant interplay that is conducive to learning. Time on task is virtually 100 percent.

A second commercial model is that of a company like Kaplan, which focuses on preparing for a wide range of standardized tests (e.g., LSAT, GRE, SAT, and ACT). The groups tend to be larger than Sylvan and they use computer simulation time to enhance achievement. Again, this program falls in the gray area between conventional instruction and tutoring.

REMEDIAL TUTORING USING STAND-ALONE PROGRAMS

This third form of tutoring is quite different from the previous two because it is focused on persons with special needs using one of a number of clearly defined remediation programs, such as the Wilson Reading System or the Laubach Literacy Program. Each of these has an extensive inventory of printed materials that provide exactly predetermined teaching activities aimed at a very particular audience. In the latter case, the target audience is teenagers and adults seeking basic instruction in reading, math, listening, writing, and speaking (Friedman et al., 2006, pp. 322–324)

A remedial tutorial program like Reading Recovery from New Zealand is focused on first graders having trouble with the initial steps in reading. It emphasizes phonics with contextual information. That is, it does not fall into the common practice of using either the phonics or whole language approach (Friedman et al., 2006, pp. 319–320).

Tutoring is the single most effective method for successful test preparation. This may be of three basic types. First, it may be the basic method of primary instruction. Second, it may be the primary method of remediation for specific areas of weakness. Third, it may take the form of application of one of a number of specific programs aimed at defined groups of learners, such as first graders struggling with the first reading steps.

REFERENCES

Alexander the Great. 2007. www.en.wikipedia.org (accessed September 10, 2007).

Aristotle. 2007. www.en.wikipedia.org (accessed September 10, 2007).

Carroll, J. B. 1963. A model of school learning. *Teachers College Record*, 64, 723–733.

Friedman, M. I., Harwell, D. H., and Schnepel, K. C. 2006. *Effective instruction: A handbook of evidence-based strategies*. Columbia, SC: Institute for Evidence-Based Decision-Making in Education.

Gordon, E. E., Morgan, R. R., O'Malley, C. J., and Ponticell, J. 2007. *The tutoring revolution: Applying research for best practices, policy implications, and student achievement*. Lanham, MD: Rowman & Littlefield.

Holt, J. 1964. *How children fail*. Dexter, MO: Delta Publishing.

Institute of Education Sciences. 2004. 1.1 million homeschooled students in the United States in 2003. Publication no. 2006042. Washington, DC: National Center for Education Statistics.

Klein, K. 2006. X = Karen (Johnny) > 95%. *Los Angeles Times*, February 4, p. B15.

Moore, R., and Moore, D. 1975. *Better late than early: A new approach to your child's education*. Pleasantville, NY: Reader's Digest Press.

National Home Education Research Institute. 2007. Welcome to the NHERI. www.nheri.org (accessed September 11, 2007).

8

Is Technology the Answer?

Today many people look to technology, and, more specifically, to computers to supply the answers to the questions in their daily lives. For test preparation, Internet resources usually are not sufficient in themselves; they are important only as far as they are able to support underlying goals. I recall a school district in South Carolina that devoted massive resources to give each high school student in the district a laptop computer. The presence of the computers alone was expected to repay the expense; however, the changes in instruction needed to utilize the hardware came slowly and painfully. In the end, providing the computers was easier than modifying instructional practice.

Some years ago, another district in South Carolina made the move to computers by purchasing a number at a steep discount. Then they sat back, thinking that they had finally made the "Big Move" and were done. However, they had purchased outdated Texas Instruments units with cassette storage drives, a quirky operating system, limited memory, and no software! Small instructional units could be written in BASIC (a simple programming language), which I did, but the overall application was impossible. Those old cassette storage devices were nothing but frustrating.

Another neighboring district, which is among the nation's poorest, went the route of adopting the PC Jr., which was similar to the personal computer that has become the industry standard but required different accessories and software. The adoption became an expensive dead end for the district, which it could ill afford.

Telephone callers often ask whether my test preparation materials are for sale. They are. The next question often reveals a problem inherent with the application of technology to test preparation. I ask the person whether he or she is able to learn content easily and effectively without a human "teacher." Most decide that they cannot do that very well. For that reason alone, technology may not be very helpful to many.

One of the best ways that the Internet can assist is by giving specific information on test content. Test makers such as the Educational Testing Service (ETS) have extensive Web sites that give broad information on registration, content, test sites, handicapped accommodations, and fees, all of which are necessary to anyone planning a personal or group preparation program. The strong tendency lately is for test publishers to move toward providing information and resources exclusively on the Internet.

ETS, which publishes a wide array of tests such as PRAXIS, SAT, and GRE, moved decisively in this direction during the period from 2002 to 2004. For many years, information was available either on the Internet or in published bulletins. Both were free. Then, in 2003, ETS began to curtail paper publications. Colleges and universities that previously received literally thousands of printed Tests at a Glance (TaaGs) now received only about a dozen. By the next year none were available and the company's transition to the Internet was nearly complete. The Information Bulletin followed. What was once a substantial sixty-six-page pamphlet was reduced to four. The overall savings to the company must have been monumental—the savings on postage alone must have been breathtaking—but it pushed customers into mandatory use of computers. There has been a similar movement by ETS toward online test registration. These tendencies have forced most persons to use computers for an increased array of test-related activities.

Some tests are actually administered by computer, or you have the option to take the test by computer. In PRAXIS the two tests you may take via computer are PRAXIS I and ParaPro. Test takers have the option to take PRAXIS I on a regularly scheduled test date with paper and pencil (PPST) or on computer at Pro-Metric or Sylvan Learning Centers (C-PPST). Both are graded on the same scale, so the same passing scores apply. The computer forms of the math and reading tests give immediate scores; the writing test scores take a few weeks because human graders must read the essays. Another advantage of the computer form is that it may be given much more often. However, for some test takers, getting immediate feedback is *not* an advantage. Imagine taking three tests and knowing you failed the first one immediately; your concentration on the last two would necessarily decrease. I imagine the security issues are also more complex than with the paper forms because the computer tests reside in computers at many locations that are available twenty-four hours a day, seven days a week.

There are also wonderful resources for specific instruction on particular pieces of test content. I recall one student who asked me where to find information on the different types of writing, such as persuasive or narrative, as she prepared for the PRAXIS test in English. I immediately went to the Trackstar Web site (www.trackstar .4teachers.org), searched on the keywords "types of writing," and found several resources that were exactly what she needed.

I have found the Trackstar Web site to be especially helpful for test preparation. It provides access to resources across many subject fields and grade levels. The filter feature is especially useful in narrowing the number of "hits" to those most relevant. A particular search can be limited to a single subject and even to particular grade levels. For example, a search on subject-verb agreement could be limited to language arts and to middle school. With the large Trackstar database of some 300,000 tracks, 849 entries (i.e., lessons) were found meeting the above criteria on a search performed on August 24, 2007. Focused information and lessons like this could be of great value for anyone needing that kind of assistance.

Another wonderful educational source now available on the Internet is the book *Effective Instruction* (Friedman et al., 2006, quoted so often in this volume), which is now available as a searchable database on the Effective Schools Web site at www.effectiveschools.com. This means that all of the information in that useful book is available on your computer, plus you have the option to enter search terms for relevant segments pertaining to particular subjects and/or grades.

As I mentioned in Chapter 2, I place great emphasis on students learning vocabulary and terms. Here also computer resources can be helpful. Some months ago I was looking at the PRAXIS II Middle School Language Arts test to locate vocabulary. In the TaaG I found dozens of terms that I entered into Wikipedia (www.en.wikipedia.org), which gave me good definitions and clear examples. In addition, it kept prompting me to look at related terms in a kind of "branching" pattern, which would have aided any person preparing for that particular test.

Many Web sites can actually provide some level of instruction on a specific skill, such as multiplying fractions or understanding pronoun-antecedent agreement. Typically they will have a demonstration of the skill and a number of practice exercises. They would serve a similar purpose to what a teacher might use in classroom instruction.

Some Web sites, such as the SAT site (www.ets.org), offer features such as the "question of the day." These allow students to practice on actual test questions. This, I believe, is not really studying and should not be relied on for significant test score improvement. However, these features provide insight into areas where a student may need to concentrate and study further. For example, if a student has trouble with word problems involving proportions, that information can guide in setting up in-depth study time on the subject.

A parallel application of technology is the use if CDs that may accompany test guidebooks. Currently both SAT and ACT study guides have these available. Generally these are sets of sample questions or complete sample tests that may be taken. Again, as above, they may be of limited value. Too many students find sets of questions too seductive and simply cannot refrain from using them extensively to study. Early in my test preparation career I used sets of test questions extensively and even checked them out to students for weeks at a time. A student from Berkley County, South Carolina, changed my mind about the efficacy of this approach when she told me at the end of the course how she loved having the questions to study. She had *memorized* the hundreds of questions in the book! She subsequently failed the test. What she (and I) had failed to realize was that if she could read a question, then it would not be on her test. After test makers like ETS release a question and let it be published or put out as a sample Internet question they do not use it again.

If my student had used the information from the sample questions differently, she probably would have passed. The only exception I know to this rule came from one of my PRAXIS secondary math students. She ordered and paid for the practice study materials from ETS. At that time, the math materials were a packet of materials and booklets and were not bound together as they are today. She studied them diligently. When she took her exam, it was *exactly* the one she had been given to study; ETS had sent her a "hot" test form by mistake instead of the "retired" one they intended. She made an excellent grade and had done nothing wrong, but ETS invalidated the test because of their error.

A more productive approach would be to do two things with sample questions:

1. Use them as a source of words, terms, symbols, and names for study.

2. Find content areas missed and focus on them for additional concentrated study.

Let's look at the second item and expand it. Say you are preparing for one of the tests that contains social studies questions. As you take sample tests, you note that you tend to miss questions on the American Civil War. Doing even more questions on the Civil War won't help because they do not tend to be systematic. You must go back and initiate a plan to study that subject. Then and only then will you be able to do better on Civil War questions.

I have also seen courses advertised on video or audio that cover specific subjects in science, history, or literature. These would seem to be good sources of concentrated review. Some seem to be derived from college lectures by highly qualified instructors, but they are not inexpensive.

An example will be illustrative. The Teaching Company (www.teach12.com) offers lectures across an array of subjects. They list topics in business, economics, fine arts, music, history, literature, English language, philosophy, intellectual history, religion, science, mathematics, and social sciences. Let me summarize their offering titled "History of Ancient Rome." The lecturer is Dr. Garrett Fagan of Pennsylvania State University. The subject is covered in forty-eight 30-minute lectures for a total of twenty-four hours of content. The formats available are:

DVD	$129.95
Audio CD	$89.95
Audio download	$64.95
Audiotape	$64.95
Transcript	$64.95

One advantage that this type of technology offers to a person undertaking systematic test preparation is that otherwise unproductive time can be used to great advantage. I can see how a person who drives a car regularly could move through a great deal of material in a few months. For example, based on a daily one-way commute of 30 minutes, all of the above material on Ancient Rome could be heard in about a month. Technology can make us more efficient.

Although not so detailed or extensive, local public libraries now offer an array of audiotapes and CDs related to many test preparation subject areas. The advantage of these materials is that there is no charge for using them. I have personally used this resource for many hundreds of hours of informative, stimulating entertainment while driving. I have listened to fascinating coverage of the Civil War and both world wars. Wonderful biographies and autobiographies are also on the shelves. I have learned much about Dwight Eisenhower, Winston Churchill, and Benjamin Franklin from audiotapes or CDs.

A clear advantage of computer instruction is that many children and adults prefer working on computers. They are highly computer literate and enjoy using that skill. You can even find preschoolers who are amazingly adept at computers! My four-year-old granddaughter appreciates any time spent on a computer and would be drawn to that approach for any kind of instruction. It may be that computers inadvertently tap into a person's control motive and that they feel more involved with every keystroke (Friedman et al., 2006, p. 238).

Another positive way that technology can impact test preparation is in the swiftness of information exchange. Students often submit questions via e-mail that I am able to answer in just a few minutes. In a similar manner, assignments such as essays or math problems can be submitted, corrected, and returned in a matter of minutes.

Another way to look at this technology issue is as Friedman et al. (2006) view it in strategy 20, "Utilizing Computerized Instruction." Implementation of computerized instruction is a great deal more than turning students loose with a computer. This resource must be integrated with the lessons to be learned. The following seven steps from the research outline that procedure.

1. Decide on an appropriate program.
2. Acquaint the students with its operation and options.
3. Decide on an appropriate individual entry point.
4. Have students proceed with the program.
5. Check that each student is making the desired progress.
6. Have students move forward to succeeding steps.
7. Repeat steps 4–6 until the desired learning has taken place. (Friedman et al., 2006, p. 240)

Another clear implication of the research is the necessity for its integration into instruction. Here prescriptions may be made and then computer work assigned.

Following computer instruction, another evaluation is made about the learning achieved and a decision is made to repeat or to move on. No research seems to support the sufficiency of computer instruction alone.

One of the advantages of using a computer is that students must give constant responses. They are prompted to respond to questions or to move to the next page. In a certain sense, computerized instruction is similar to one-on-one tutoring. In both, constant responses are required. A second advantage of using a computer is that it is tireless; it will repeat a question or give a correction again and again. It does not lose patience or good humor, as a live teacher or tutor might.

Perhaps the best answer to the question posed in the title of this chapter, "Is technology the answer?" is that it is not *the* answer, but it can be part of the answer.

REFERENCE

Friedman, M. I., Harwell, D. H., and Schnepel, K. C. 2006. *Effective instruction: A handbook of evidence-based strategies*. Columbia, SC: Institute for Evidence-Based Decision-Making in Education.

9

Conclusion

Test performance can be enhanced by providing a program that addresses a wide array of concerns, from the purely physical to the purely cognitive. These concerns include:

Health improvement

Anxiety reduction

Reading improvement

Learning and implementing test-taking strategies

Test content review

Vocabulary enhancement

Quality of instruction improved

Time devoted to instruction increased

I conclude this volume with a personal note from one of my students regarding her results on the August 2007 PRAXIS administration test. Her e-mail references many of the approaches that I have discussed in the previous chapters.

Dr. Hatch!

What can I say? You have done it again! This time in one day! I attended your session on August 1, 2007 at USC-Sumter to be ready for the August 4 tests, and taking your class that day—learning how to read the graphs, how to answer the questions, understanding how they score the tests, exercising, keeping my mouth shut the day of the test—along with my previous studying, it finally paid off! Thank you, Thank you, Thank you!

Now I had not received my scores in the mail yet, so I had to call because the last day for registering was August 31. Therefore I called for my scores on

Friday and don't you know, Doc, Friday was my birthday? The customer service rep from ETS said, "Mrs. _____, you are going to have a Happy Birthday!" My score on the administration was 680. I only needed a 590. Even though I am better on multiple-choice tests, the even higher score was due to an understanding of those graphs that you told me would show up on that test. And my score on the PLT, where I needed a 165, was a 166! Whew!!!! I barely made it, but I made it! Doc, on my previous tests my highest score was a 150, so I made great gains just being in your class that Wednesday evening. I also must share that the day of test and taking the PLT, I had no anxiety. I was at peace with myself. Why? Because I had an understanding. I am a Christian and I know God sent me to you in the nick of time and I give Him all the praises for you assisting me in becoming a professional teacher. You helped me with all my tests (remember the Business Education—I only needed a 540 and I made a 610). The reason why it took me so long to pursue my calling in becoming a teacher was my fear of taking these tests. Now I can teach with peace!

Doc, I have been so excited and I told all of my administrators, "Thank God for Dr. Hatch." There's one more teacher who needs to attend your class and I will make sure he gets into your class. Doc, one day, if the Lord wills, I want to help others like you have done for me! A lot of teachers are not teachers today because they have not passed the PLT. I am definitely going to promote your workshops!

Thanks so much again and may God bless you and your family richly!

Sincerely,

[Student name]

Florence (SC) School District 4 (Personal communication, September 4, 2007, reprinted with permission)

Appendix: Essay Feedback Sheet

CWH Consulting Co. Inc.
1250 Jones St.
Newberry, SC 29108
803-276-8887

ESSAY FEEDBACK SHEET

KEY: Satisfactory − S; Poor = P; Yes = Y; No = N

APPEARANCE	Margins (left and right)	S	P
	Handwriting	S	P
STRUCTURE	Outline (present)	Y	N
	Outline (used)	Y	N
	5 Paragraphs	Y	N
	4 Sentences/paragraph	Y	N
Introduction (First Paragraph)	Clear Presentation	Y	N
	Confined to 1 idea	Y	N
Idea One (Second Paragraph)	Clear Presentation	Y	N
	Confined to 1 idea	Y	N
Idea Two (Third Paragraph)	Clear Presentation	Y	N
	Confined to 1 idea	Y	N
Idea Three (Fourth Paragraph)	Clear Presentation	Y	N
	Confined to 1 idea	Y	N

Conclusion (Fifth Paragraph)	Clear Presentation	Y	N
	Confined to 1 idea	Y	N

IMAGES
    Writing uses good, clear images and examples   Y N

MECHANICS

SPELLING	S	P
GRAMMAR	S	P
Subject-Verb Agreement	S	P
Pronoun-Antecedent Agreement	S	P
Avoidance of Sentence Fragments	S	P
Lack of Homonym Problems	S	P
(Example: there, their, they're)		
Formation of Possessives and Contractions	S	P
(Example: men's, Charles', it's)		
Nouns, Correct Formation of Plurals	S	P
Verbs, Correct Formations, -ed, -ing, -s	S	P

On a scale of 0–12 (like PRAXIS) this would probably be about _____

Fix and return? Y N   Send me another? Y N

Bibliography

Action for Healthy Kids. 2004. The role of sound nutrition and physical activity in academic achievement. www.actionforhealthykids.org (accessed August 18, 2006).

Alaimo, K. et al. 2001. Food insufficiency and American school-aged children's cognitive, academic and psychosocial development. *Pediatrics*, 108(1), 44–53.

Alexander the Great. 2007. www.en.wikipedia.org (accessed September 10, 2007).

American School Food Service Association. 1989. Impact of hunger and malnutrition on school achievement. *School Board Food Service Research Review*, 1(Spring), 17–20.

Anderson, L. W. 1995. Time, allocated, and instructional. In L. W. Anderson (Ed.), *International encyclopedia of teaching and teacher education* (2nd ed., pp. 204–207). Oxford: Pergamon Press.

Aristotle. 2007. www.en.wikipedia.org (accessed September 10, 2007).

Bobrow, J. 1985. *Cliffs math review for standardized tests*. New York: Wiley.

Brown, L. et al. 1996. Malnutrition, poverty and intellectual development. *Scientific American*, 274(2), 38–43.

Carroll, J. B. 1963. A model of school learning. *Teachers College Record*, 64, 723–733.

Center on Hunger, Poverty and Nutrition Policy. 1995. Statement on the link between nutrition and cognitive development in children. Medford, MA: Tufts University.

The College Board. 2001a. *A historical perspective on the SAT 1926–2001*. Princeton, NJ: College Board SAT Program.

The College Board. 2001b. *Predicting success in college: SAT studies of classes graduating since 1980*. Princeton, NJ: College Board SAT Program.

Compuserve. 2007. Read this: You'll start exercising today. What's New, www.compuserve.com (accessed September 7, 2007).

Covino, W. A., and Orton, P. Z. 1986. *Cliffs verbal review for standardized tests*. New York: Wiley.

Darling-Hammond, L. 1999. Teacher quality and student achievement: A review of state policy evidence. Document R-99-1. Seattle, WA: Center for the Study of Teaching and Policy.

Dewalt, M. W. 2006. *Amish education in the United States and Canada*. Lanham, MD: Rowman & Littlefield.

Epstein, L., and Mardon, S. 2007. Homeroom zombies. *Newsweek*, 150(12), September 17, 64–65.

Fitzsimons, G., and Williams, P. 2000. Asking questions can change choice behavior: Does it do so automatically or effortfully? *Journal of Experimental Psychology: Applied*, 6(3), 195–206.

Friedman, M. I., Harwell, D. H., and Schnepel, K. C. 2006. *Effective instruction: A handbook of evidence-based strategies.* Columbia, SC: Institute for Evidence-Based Decision-Making in Education.

Friedman, M. I. et al. 2003. *Educators' handbook on effective testing.* Columbia, SC: Institute for Evidence-Based Decision-Making in Education.

Gagne, R. M. 1962. The acquisition of knowledge. *Psychological Review*, 69(4), 355–365.

Gordon, E. E., Morgan, R. R., O'Malley, C. J., and Ponticell, J. 2007. *The tutoring revolution: Applying research for best practices, policy implications, and student achievement.* Lanham, MD: Rowman & Littlefield.

Harvard School of Public Health. 2006. Exercise. www.harvard.edu/nutritionsource/exercise (accessed August 18, 2006).

Hawkes, B., ed. 1999. *Guide to standardized test preparation.* Upper Saddle River, NJ: Globe Fearon.

Holt, J. 1964. *How children fail.* Dexter, MO: Delta Publishing.

Institute of Education Sciences. 2004. 1.1 million homeschooled students in the United States in 2003. Publication no. 2006042. Washington, DC: National Center for Education Statistics.

Klein, K. 2006. X = Karen (Johnny) > 95%. *Los Angeles Times*, February 4, p. B15.

Lee, I. M. et al. 2003. Relative intensity of physical exercise and risk of coronary heart disease. *Circulation*, 107, 1110–1116.

Manson, J. E. et al. 1999. A prospective study of walking as compared with vigorous exercise in the prevention of coronary heart disease in women. *New England Journal of Medicine*, 341(9), 650–658.

Mental Measurements Yearbook. Various years. Lincoln, NE: Buros Institute.

Mitchell, K. J. et al. 2001. *Testing teacher candidates: The role of licensure tests in improving teacher quality.* Washington, DC: National Academy Press.

Moore, R., and Moore, D. 1975. *Better late than early: A new approach to your child's education.* Pleasantville, NY: Reader's Digest Press.

National Home Education Research Institute. 2007. Welcome to the NHERI. www.nheri.org (accessed September 11, 2007).

Netscape News. 2006a. The no. 1 skill teens need for college. www.netscape.compuserve.com (accessed October 9, 2006).

Netscape News. 2006b. Uh oh: Dire effect of skimping on sleep. www.netscape.compuserve.com (accessed October 24, 2006).

Netscape News. 2007. Top 5 consequences of too-little sleep. www.netscape.compuserve.com (accessed November 7, 2007).

Netscape What's New. 2007. Diet drinks: Scary warning! www.netscape.compuserve.com (accessed September 2, 2007).

The new class struggle: Hang up and learn. 2007. *State Newspaper* (Columbia, SC), November 9, p. A11.

Parker, L. 1989. *The relationship between nutrition and learning: A school employee's guide to information and action.* Washington, DC: National Education Association.

Pollitt, E. et al. 1991. Brief fasting, stress, and cognition in children. *American Journal of Clinical Nutrition*, 34(August), 1526–1533.

Powers, D. E., and Rock, D. A. 1998. Effect of coaching on SAT I: Reasoning scores. College Board Report 98-6. Princeton, NJ: College Board.

Rosenthal, R., and Jacobson, L. 1992. *Pygmalion in the classroom: Teacher expectations and pupils' intellectual development*. New York: Irvington Publishers.

Schmelzer, R. V. 1992. *Reading and study skills*. Reading Rate Boosters, Book Two. Dubuque, IA: Kendall/Hunt.

Schmelzer, R. V., and Christen, W. L. 1996. *Reading and study skills*. [Revised edition.] Reading Rate Boosters, Book One. Dubuque, IA: Kendall/Hunt. (Originally published in 1980.)

Schoenthaler, S. et al. 1991. Controlled trial of vitamin supplementation: Effects on intelligence and performance. *Personality and Individual Differences*, 12(4), 361.

Sprott, D. E. et al. 2006. The question-behavior effect: What we know and where we go from here. *Social Influence*, 1(2), 128–137.

Study ties food additives, hyperactivity in children. 2007. *State Newspaper* (Columbia, SC), September 7, p. A7.

Women's math skills linked to expectations. 2005. *State Newspaper* (Columbia, SC), October 20, p. A14.

Index

About the Author

CHARLES W. HATCH, Ph.D. is President of CWH Consulting Company, Newberry, South Carolina. He earned a Master of Arts in Teaching at Johns Hopkins University and a doctorate in Educational Research and Measurement at the University of South Carolina. He has taught college courses in tests and measurement, statistics, and test preparation. Dr. Hatch has published the "Introductory Handbook of Measurement," "An Introductory Handbook for Statistical Package Programming," and papers on the subject of predicting freshman retention. He has served as a consultant on test preparation, college retention, and microcomputers and software.

Dr. Hatch is affiliated with the Friedman Institute for Evidence-Based Decision-Making in Education (EDIE) and coauthored the *Educators' Handbook on Effective Testing* (2003) with Dr. Myles Friedman et al.

Dr. Hatch and his wife, Fran, live in Newberry, South Carolina, and are the proud parents of two children, Lisa and David, and three granddaughters, Samantha, Kimberly, and Robin.